Modern Bulgarian Literature

The History of

Modern
Bulgarian
Literature

by

CLARENCE A. MANNING
and
ROMAN SMAL-STOCKI

GREENWOOD PRESS, PUBLISHERS
WESTPORT, CONNECTICUT

Library of Congress Cataloging in Publication Data

Manning, Clarence Augustus, 1893-
    The history of modern Bulgarian literature.

    Reprint of the ed. published by Bookman Associates,
New York.
    Bibliography: p.
    1. Bulgarian literature--History and criticism.
I. Smal-Stocki, Roman, 1893-   joint author.
II. Title.
[PG1008.M3 1974]   891.8'1'09   73-21262
ISBN 0-8371-6130-4

Foreword

This outline of modern Bulgarian literature is the result of an exchange of memories of Bulgaria between the authors some years ago in New York.

We both have visited Bulgaria many times, we have had many personal friends among its scholars and statesmen, and we feel a deep sympathy for the tragic plight of this long-suffering Slavic nation with its industrious and hard-working people.

We both feel also that it is an injustice to Bulgaria and a loss to American Slavic scholarship that, in spite of the importance of Bulgaria for the Slavic world, so little attention is paid to the country's cultural contributions. This is the more deplorable for American influence in Bulgaria was great, even before World War I. Many Bulgarians were educated in Robert College in Constantinople and after World War I in the American College in Sofia, one of the institutions supported by the Near East Foundation. Many Bulgarian professors have visited the United States in happier times. So it seems unfair that Americans and American universities have ignored so completely the development of the Bulgarian genius and culture during the past century.

Even American Slavic scholars know little or nothing of modern Bulgarian literature. There have been a few translations of the works of two of the greatest authors, Khristo Botev and Ivan Vazov, but these are now out of print. The other nineteenth- and twentieth-century authors are not even known by name in the United States. In short, any attempts to interpret Bulgarian literary culture have been either non-existent or so feeble that they have scarcely achieved their purpose of making the country known in the Anglo-Saxon world.

Yet modern Bulgarian literature, from its scanty origins in the eighteenth century, has developed an individuality which differentiates it from the culture of the other Slavic nations and corresponds to the Bulgarian national character and to the unfortunate fate of the Bulgarian nation. The nation was forced to enter two World Wars on the losing side and, now under the terror of the Communists, it is under a government that is intent upon changing the entire traditional culture of the people and upon remodelling its customs and literature according to the Soviet pattern.

It is our modest aim to help fill this vacuum in America with this study of modern Bulgarian literature, presented against the background of Bulgarian history, which offers a good example of the evolution of modern Slavic nationalism. We sincerely hope that this volume will lead to a better understanding of the path which the Bulgarians have been compelled to travel. We believe that it will give a better understanding to the people and encourage efforts to set the Bulgarian people free from their present yoke to resume their march toward membership in a free world and a world of peace, harmony, freedom, and democracy for all nations.

At the present moment literary research in both Bulgaria and the Soviet Union is stressing the interrelations of Bulgarian and Ukrainian literature. These relationships have been almost completely disregarded by American scholars and so they have been more or less noted in this volume. As the Ukrainian authors are little known to Americans, footnotes have been appended for purposes of identification.

In the last chapter we have added selections of Bulgarian poetry, for poetry is one of the most characteristic features of any literature.

The transliteration system used in this book is based upon that of the Library of Congress with some necessary modifications.

To differentiate the ancient state of Kievan Rus from the rising Principality of Moscow, we have used for the former the term found in the works of Geoffrey Chaucer, the medieval English word, "Ruce."

In conclusion we can only hope that in some degree this book will serve its purpose of making known to the American people a Slavic country which has had a remarkable and unfortunate history but which is still far from conquered and will ultimately play its own free role in the free world.

New York, New York
Milwaukee, Wisconsin
October, 1958

CLARENCE A. MANNING
ROMAN SMAL-STOCKI

Contents

Chapter   *Page*

1. The Historical Background   11
2. Old and Middle Bulgarian Literature   30
3. Father Paisi Khilandarski   45
4. Educators and Revolutionists   52
5. Khristo Botev   73
6. Ivan Vazov   80
7. The First Decades after Liberation   94
8. The Coming of Modernism   107
9. Bulgarian Prose and Drama   123
10. The Period of Discouragement   130
11. Toward Communism   145
12. The Communist Period   152
Conclusion The Characteristics of Bulgarian Literature   163

Selections of Bulgarian Poetry   167

    Bulgarian Folksongs   167

    Petko Rachev Slaveykov   171

    Khristo Botev   174

    Ivan Vazov   177

    Pencho Slaveykov   181

    Peyu Yavorov   184

Notes   187

Selected Bibliography   190

Index   192

CHAPTER ONE

The Historical Background

To understand the special situation in which modern Bulgarian literature developed, we must have at least a general idea of the history of the Bulgarian people in the past as well as in the present. We must take into account the geographical position of the land which likewise played an important role in the fate of the nation.

The Bulgarian people, numbering almost 7,000,000, live in the eastern half of the Balkan peninsula and occupy much of the area in which the original Bulgarians first settled. Their territory is bounded on the east by the Black Sea and the European section of Turkey. In the south Greek Thrace, a narrow strip of territory which was once under Bulgarian rule, cuts them off from the Aegean Sea. In the west their territory abuts on Yugoslavia. The northern boundary of the state is the Danube River which separates them from Romania and near its delta creates the thorny Dobrudja question. The territory is cut almost in half by the Balkan Mountains with the fertile lands to the north sloping down to the Danube and those of the south toward the Greek border.

The territory which the Bulgarians now inhabit was formerly a part of the Roman Empire and the course of the old Roman roads can still be traced, especially those running from the west to the east. With the division of the Roman Empire in the year 395, the present Bulgarian lands fell within the territory of the Eastern Empire with its political and ecclesiastical capital at Constantinople or, as the Greeks liked to call it, "New Rome." This territory was then largely inhabited by Greeks, although it undoubtedly contained remnants of the pre-Greek

11

Thracians and Illyrians. These latter peoples, of whom we have little detailed knowledge, flowed over into Macedonia, originally the homeland of Philip and Alexander the Great.

In the course of the sixth century this area was invaded by various East Slavic tribes, partly the ancestors of the present-day Belo-Ruthenians and Ukrainians, who overran the Balkan Peninsula and even settled in the Peloponnesus.[1] At that time the entire territory from Mount Haemus to the Peloponnesus and the Aegean Sea was called Slavania or Slavonia.[2] How far these Slavs accepted Christianity is still uncertain but there was apparently little conflict at this period between the old inhabitants and the invaders. They were well on their way to being acclimated in the Byzantine Empire when the Bulgarian horde[3] made its appearance.

This was a group of Altaic-speaking nomads, and their language was probably a mixture of Turkic dialects with some possible influences of the old Hunnic speech, something like modern Chuvash. They formed the nucleus of a state on the Volga in Black Bulgary where their leaders showed remarkable statesmanship. In the course of the seventh century, during the folk migrations, they moved westward across the Ukraine and into the present Romania. Finally, in 679, under Khan Asperukh, they crossed the Danube into the old province of Moesia. Following wars with the Byzantines, they secured permission of the Byzantine Emperor to establish a Bulgarian state with its first capital at Pliska-Aboba in the northeastern part of modern Bulgaria. Since this was about the time when Constantinople was threatened by the first great assault of the Arabs, some scholars have thought that the Bulgarian horde had some understanding with the other foes of Byzantium.

For the next two centuries Bulgaria prospered. The Slavic cultivators, a sturdy and hard-working stock, soon Slavicized the Bulgarian nomads who formed a comparatively small dominant class. Giving up its nomadic habits, the horde merged with the surrounding Slavs and by intermarriage created a unified Slavic nation under the old Altaic name. By the beginning of the ninth century, even the original Bulgarian Altaic language had disappeared and had been replaced by a form of

Slavic. The process was similar to that which went on when the Franks, the Teutonic conquerors of Gaul, were completely assimilated by the native population but left the country and nation their name—France. In Bulgaria, too, the conquerors, the Altaic Bulgars, gave their name to the more civilized Slavic tribes whose customs and language they adopted. During these centuries the state expanded to the south and west and included the area around Lake Okhrida in the western part of the Balkans. Next to the Byzantine Empire, it was the strongest state in south central Europe and its borders nearly touched those of another Slavic country, the still inchoate Great Moravian Empire (836-907) which the Slovaks claim as their mothercountry.

The history of the new Slavic state of Bulgaria was greatly influenced by its geopolitical situation: (1) It was located on the largest and longest European river and its delta, the Danube, which from the earliest times had been a highroad for commercial and military movements between the west and the east, between Europe, the Dardanelles and Asia. Along this route Bulgaria dominated the Balkan Mountains and so it controlled passage from Constantinople to central Europe by land. (2) The most sensitive spot on this Danube-Black Sea route to Asia was the Dardanelles which connected the eastern Mediterranean basin with the Black Sea and thus formed a north-south route which was extended by the Dnieper waterway deep into eastern Europe and furnished a convenient access to the Baltic Sea and northern Europe. Thus Constantinople and the Dardanelles, at the junction of these two routes, were in a position of world importance in politics and commerce and affected the history of three continents, Europe, Asia and Africa. It is therefore no accident that this region was the scene of the Trojan War which inspired the first great work of world literature, Homer's *Iliad.* (3) Bulgaria, with its borders on the Black Sea, was a part of the entire Black Sea complex, which was the meeting point of different cultures, races and religious movements from Iranian, Caucasian and Asiatic sources, as well as a part of the old classical world. The Greeks had commenced to colonize the Black Sea coasts in 700 B.C., made of them a Greek province and implanted their cultural supremacy for the next millenium. Moreover, through the northern part of this Black Sea complex ran the great continental highway from Asia into Europe through the "Gate of Peoples" between the Caspian Sea and the Ural Mountains. Over this route had passed the invasions of the Huns, the Avars, the Tatars, the Hungarians, and the smaller invasion of the Bulgarians which resulted in the formation of Bulgaria. This route crossed the extension of the north-south route at Kiev in Ukraine and so the Black Sea coast of Bulgaria was included in nearly all the movements that emanated from Constantinople or affected it from the East and West.

There were few periods of friendly relations between Constantinople and the Bulgarians and every step in the growth of Bulgaria was marked by bitter struggle. Thus in 811 Khan Krum, who had moved his capital to Preslav (the Roman Marcianopolis) a few miles from Pliska-Aboba, succeeded in defeating and killing the Emperor Nicephorus. Following the old Asiatic custom of the original Bulgars, he used the Emperor's skull as a drinking cup to celebrate his victory.

Paganism still continued, especially among the ruling class of the khanate, but in the middle of the ninth century Khan Boris (852-889) apparently saw the advantages of regularizing his position and gaining Christian support by adopting Christianity as the religion of his state and he used King Louis the German as a mediator with Rome. He sought ecclesiastical autonomy from Rome as well as from Constantinople and he wanted his own Bulgarian hierarch. Under pressure from Emperor Michael III, he ultimately turned to Constantinople and accepted Christianity but he had to accept a Greek archbishop and somewhat less autonomy than he had desired. Bulgaria then became the object of a protracted struggle between Rome and Constantinople as both sought jurisdiction over the Bulgarian Church.[4]

At almost the same time Prince Rostislav (846-870) of the Great Moravian state felt himself menaced by the advance of German Christianity and appealed in 863 to Constantinople for Slavic-speaking missionaries. The Patriarch Photius sent two,

Constantine the Philosopher and his brother, the monk Methodius, to preach Slavic Christianity in Moravia. These two brothers, the founders of the Slavic Liturgy, were already distinguished men. They had spoken the Slavic of the Bulgarian hinterland of Salonika from childhood and had untertaken various diplomatic missions in the East for the Emperor and the Church. Now in preparation for their new mission, Constantine, the more intellectual of the two brothers, with a fine general philosophical and theological background, drew up an alphabet for the Slavic language and prepared a Slavic translation of the Liturgy and other church books. The Byzantine Emperor, Michael III, in sending the two brothers to Rostislav, was fully aware of the historical importance of this new Bulgarian alphabet and the Slavic books for divine service, and evaluated them as follows in his letter to Rostislav: "Receive this gift, greater and more valuable than all gold and silver, precious stones, and transitory riches."[5] The mission of the brothers prospered but as they were bitterly denounced by the German missionaries, they decided that it would be better to seek the approval of the Pope for the Slavic Liturgy. They went to Rome in the year 867 and secured the approval of the Slavic Liturgy by Pope Hadrian II. In 869 Constantine died in Rome after becoming a monk under the name of Cyril. He was buried in Rome in the Church of St. Clement. Hence the brothers, later canonized, are usually referred to as Saints Cyril and Methodius.[6] The Moravian mission spread also in Bohemia. One centre was the Sazava Monastery which was liquidated in 1097. It reached Poland where the first Metropolitan See was of the Slavic Rite (located, after 922, probably in Sandomierz).[7] Methodius and his successors are also credited with the beginnings of Christianity in Ukrainian Volynia[8] and in the whole of Ruce-Ukraine.[9]

Finally after many persecutions at the hands of the Germans, St. Methodius died in 885 and his disciples were forced to leave Moravia. Some went into Western Ruce-Ukraine and some returned to Bulgaria where St. Clement settled at Okhrida in the west and St. Naum at Preslav in the east with the support of the already Christian Boris. Thus Bulgaria became the centre for the Liturgy celebrated in that Slavic language which they had worked out as the liturgical and literary language for all the Slavs. Bulgaria became in the next decades the center of culture, learning and education for all the Southern and Eastern Slav nations and their churches. Since the Slav languages were still not so far differentiated as they are today, this Bulgarian church language was easily understood and accepted as a kind of a "high style" in all the Slavic vernaculars.

Under Boris and his son, Emperor Simeon (893-927), Bulgaria reached the height of its power.[10] The reign of Simeon was marked by extensive cultural development and both at Okhrida and Preslav there were flourishing schools of translators who made accessible to the new Slavic Christians in their own tongue many of the best works of Christian Greek thought. Bulgaria grew in power and the Bulgarian Emperors felt themselves potential rivals and challengers for the imperial throne of the East in Constantinople. As a matter of fact, the Byzantine Emperor at one time even agreed to pay an annual tribute to Bulgaria.

Thus in Bulgaria on the Slavic ethnographic border with the Byzantine Greek Empire there was laid the foundation for a Bulgarian Slavic nationalism nurtured by the political and religious clashes between Bulgaria and the Byzantine Empire, its Greek national church and civilization. The Slavic Bulgarian Empire near Byzantium tried to consolidate the Slavs of the Balkans. The proclamation of the Slavic Bulgarian language as the official language of the Bulgarian Church and its dedication to the Divine Service by the Bulgarian National Assembly (893) were of revolutionary importance and are regarded as a contribution of the Bulgarians to the whole of the Slavic world. The introduction of the Old Bulgarian language into the Church was a decisive victory over the partisans of the "three language monopoly," who held that only Hebrew, Greek and Latin were worthy of use in glorifying God. The Bulgarian Church from its very foundation identified itself with the Bulgarian national consciousness, which aspired to the leadership of the Slavic Christian world by creating a Slavic literature and culture to rival Greek and Latin.

After Simeon's death, a succession of less able rulers lost their political advantage and the center of Bulgarian political life gravitated from Preslav to the west. Europe was at this time in the Viking Age and the Norman-Vikings along the west coast of Europe and in the east along the Dnieper drove toward Constantinople, which was the chief center of civilization in the medieval world after the capture of Rome by Alaric the Goth (410). The Viking dynasty of Ruce-Ukraine, especially during the reign of Svyatoslav (962-972), included Bulgaria in its imperial plans to control Transcaucasia and Constantinople after a number of previous direct assaults upon the imperial capital. Svyatoslav (965) stormed the city of Bulgar on the Volga, the capital of the Altaic-speaking Bulgarians (Bolgarians) who still remained in the East, and in 967 invaded Bulgaria with 40,000 men. He established his capital at Pereyaslavets (Little Preslav), a fortress commanding the Danubian delta, and planned to transfer his own capital to it from Kiev. He made an alliance with Byzantium which feared the growing power of Bulgaria but, in the face of Svyatoslav's expanding ambitions, the Bulgarians and their Byzantine rivals settled their differences and combined against Svyatoslav. He was defeated in 972, gave up his claims on Bulgaria and met an untimely death on his way back to Ukraine.[11] Thus ended Svyatoslav's attempt to establish a huge Ruce-Slavic Empire with Bulgaria as a cornerstone.[12]

Tsar Samuel, who, according to tradition, was asked by the Kievan Grand Prince Volodymyr to send him priests and books, a request that was promptly granted, tried to revive Bulgarian power. He found himself opposed to one of the greater Byzantine Emperors, Basil the Macedonian, who in 1014 decisively defeated him and avenged the former imperial defeat of Nicephorus by blinding 15,000 Bulgarian prisoners and winning the title of Basil the Bulgar-Slayer (Bulgaroktonos). This cruel vengance left deep traces on the attitude of the Christian Bulgarians toward the Christian Greeks. Samuel died from the blow, and within four years the once powerful Bulgarian Empire had ceased to exist.

With the destruction of the Bulgarian state, the Bulgarian Church fell under the control of Greek ecclesiastics who took over the see of Okhrida and tried with some success to eliminate the Slavic Liturgy of SS. Cyril and Methodius and to replace it with the Liturgy in the Greek language. They could not hope to succeed, for the Slavic Liturgy had already been introduced, through Kievan Ruce-Ukraine, to the Eastern Slavs and also to Serbia and in part to Croatia, and it had been accepted as standard for the Slavic Christians of those lands. The first Eastern Slavic saints, SS. Boris and Hlib (Gleb), the murdered sons of Grand Prince Volodymyr, had a Bulgarian mother, according to the *Book of Annals,* and thus formed a link in the Church Slavic tradition.

During the tenth and eleventh centuries, as the Bulgarian power was fading, part of the peasantry drifted over into Bogomilism, a strange mixture of Christian and Iranian dualistic ideas. There is no doubt that Bogomilism was a powerful movement. It was definitely pacifistic, ascetic, and anti-ecclesiastical and, in fact, it was a kind of Christian anarchism. It recognized no authority, spiritual or civil, and openly preached disobedience. Its adherents simply hated kings, had only contempt for the elders, attacked the rich boyars (the nobility) and incited the peasants to cease working for their masters and to seek the salvation of their souls by living as vegetarians and abstaining from all normal modes of life including marriage and family. Bogomilism had some connection with the long series of dualistic movements such as Manicheanism, Paulicianism, and Massilianism that plagued the Christian world for centuries and produced a large number of apocryphal tales which found wide circulation throughout the Bulgarian sphere of influence. The movement spread westward through merchants and students and was reflected in the strange cults of the Albigenses or Bulgari (the French invective *bougre* is derived from Bugri-Bulgari) in southern France, the Cathari in Germany and England, and similar movements. Some scholars regard the Bogomils as forerunners of the Reformation in Central Europe and their efforts as a struggle of democracy against aristocracy and a fight for freedom against feudalism.[13] The Bogomil movement undermined the Bulgarian state and nation, and later the Bogomil anarchists refused to oppose the invading Turks and thus betrayed their nation.

In 1185 Ivan and Peter Asen of Tirnovo led a general revolt of the Bulgarians and the Vlachs against the Byzantine Empire and were able to establish a new state, the Second Bulgarian Empire, with its capital in Tirnovo. Like Boris, the new rulers, in their efforts to free themselves from the ecclesiastical control of Constantinople, appealed to the Pope, who formally conferred the crown upon Kaloioannes, or Kaloyan (1197-1207), the third of the dynasty. However, it was not long before an Orthodox Patriarch, Ioakhim, proclaimed again the independence of the Bulgarian Church from Constantinople at Tirnovo, and the bulk of the population remained Slavic Orthodox.

Under the Asen monarchs, the empire flourished and reached a high point of prosperity and culture, thanks to the successful diplomacy of the monarchs and their alliance with the Cumans north of the Danube. The Cumans were able to give the state considerable help during the stormy days when the Byzantine Empire fell under the control of Latin monarchs after the Fourth Crusade in 1204. The Asen monarchs continued to foster the idea of Slavic union and solidarity created by Simeon. To strengthen this union Emperor Michael Asen (1246-1257) married the daughter of Rostislav, the pretender to the throne of the Ukrainian Halych-Volynia.[14] The Asens made Tirnovo an important city with many palaces and churches, and gained for the city its prestige as a center of culture and tradition in Bulgaria, a position it has retained ever since.

When the dynasty died out in 1257, their successors were feeble and the state soon became part of the Serbian Empire of Stefan Dushan (1330), but this did not survive the death of its founder and only paved the way for the Turkish conquest in the latter part of the fourteenth century.

In 1371 the Turks defeated and killed Vukashin, one of the successors of Dushan, in a battle on the Maritsa River. This opened the way to the seizure by the Turks of Sofia and Plovdiv. Then the defeat of Knez (Prince) Lazar and the Serbs at Kosovo in 1389 destroyed the Christian resistance in the central part of the Balkan Peninsula. Two years later, in 1391, the Turks captured Tirnovo and killed the last Bulgarian emperor, Ivan Shishman. Although Bulgarian resistance continued, in 1396 with the capture by the Turks of Vidin on the Danube, fighting ceased and Bulgarian independence was lost and was not regained for nearly five centuries.

The occupation of Bulgaria by the Mohammedan Turks and its absorption into the Ottoman Empire brought great changes in the life of the Bulgarian people, especially after the fall of Constantinople (1453). During its long career the mighty Byzantine Empire had enjoyed its glorious moments but by its "cesaropapism" it had also created an unsurpassable record of corruption, cruelty, and cynicism. Of eighty emperors, ten were forced to abandon their thrones, four were imprisoned, seven blinded, and fifteen murdered.

As the Empire shrank, it was no wonder that the early Bulgarian rulers regarded the Empire with its strategically important capital as the necessary goal of their own growing state. Yet the problem of whether Constantinople would remain Greek or become Slavic Bulgarian was finally decided by the Turks who made it the political center of Islam. The rivalry of the Greeks and Bulgarians brought it about that no Slavic Orthodox people played any role in the last struggle. The alliance of Catholic France (1528) with the Sultan-Caliph against the Catholic Emperor of the Holy Roman Empire showed the same disintegration of all Christian sense of solidarity in the Catholic camp.

At the beginning of the occupation the Turkish administration was long compelled to employ the Bulgarian Church language as an official medium and many documents of the Sultan sent to Serbia, Bosnia, Bulgaria, Poland, Ukraine and Moldavia were written in this language. Many Slavs who betrayed their religion and jumped on the bandwagon of victorious Islam were employed by the Turks. Numbers of Slavs in Bulgaria and elsewhere deliberately adopted the new faith to preserve their personal estates and to secure the privileges granted by the Ottoman Empire to members of the ruling faith. Yet, on the whole the Turks preferred that their subjects should remain Christian, while they themselves kept superior military power. They made no consistent effort to amalgamate the Greeks, the Bulgarians or any other Orthodox people with themselves. The Turks preferred to leave the subject peoples to their own devices and to content themselves with the fruits of exploitation. This policy of the Turks produced curious and unexpected results after the fall of Constantinople. The last emperor of the Byzantine Empire, Constantine XI Paleologue, died courageously defending the walls of the city. His family escaped to the West and one of his nieces, Zoe, later married, under the Orthodox name of Sophia, the Grand Duke of Muscovy Ivan III. Ivan forthwith adopted the double-headed eagle of Byzantium and claimed by inheritance all the rights of the Emperors of Constantinople.

The Greeks in the Empire from the time of Constantine and the founding of the imperial city had not called themselves Greeks or Hellenes but Romans or *Romaioi* and now in their decline they still continued to use this name for themselves. They were headed by the Patriarch of Constantinople who since the sixth century had taken the title of Oecumenical Patriarch (World Patriarch). Despite the blows of Islam and the loss of the venerable Cathedral of Hagia Sophia, which the Turks turned into a mosque, the Patriarchate survived with its staff and its institutions for preserving the old Greek learning. It retreated into the interior quarter of the Phanar (phanar—lighthouse) on the upper part of the Golden Horn, adopting a policy of collaboration with the Sultan and attempting, despite all humiliations, to hold the same attitude toward the Sultan as toward the Christian emperors. The Greeks, better educated than the Turks, soon came to form a diplomatic élite in the Empire just as the Armenians came to form a financial aristocracy.

To organize and govern their conquests, the Turks created an organization for all the Christians in the Empire, the Roummillet (derived from *Romaioi*). They placed at its head the Patriarch of Constantinople and recognized him as the political head of all Orthodox Christians and gave him the right to impose taxes upon Christians for the support of the Patriarchate.

The Turks themselves executed without question the legal decisions of the Patriarchate, as long as these decisions did not infringe upon the rights of the Turks or Islam. However, by changing the Patriarch continually and exacting enormous sums of money for the appointment of a successor, they saw to it that the affairs of the Patriarchate did not prosper too well. In the seventeenth century there were fifty-five changes of patriarchs, the same man being appointed and deposed several times depending upon the political and financial whims of the Grand Viziers.

This could not fail to have a demoralizing effect upon the ecclesiastics of the Phanar and upon the laymen around them. The constant need for money to satisfy the Turks led to exactions on the people and a willingness to sacrifice everything for money. Consequently in the eyes of the subject populations and of Europe as a whole the Phanar became synonymous with greed and avarice. It could scarcely be otherwise and we can only marvel that the general moral decay was not worse than it was.

From the end of the seventeenth century the Patriarchate became even more aggressively Greek and consciously bent all its efforts toward the Hellenization of all the Orthodox Christians in the Ottoman Empire. It set itself to abolish the Church Slavic language in the service of the Church, to Hellenize all the dioceses, the ecclesiastics, and the more prominent classes of the population and to wipe out all non-Greek nationalisms in the Empire. It wished to Hellenize the Christian Balkan peoples and use them to crush the Ottoman Empire from within and to re-establish the old Greek Eastern Roman Empire. This process weighed more heavily upon the Bulgarians than upon the other Balkan peoples, for they were the nearest to the capital and hence most accessible as a source of funds.

The destruction of the Second Bulgarian Empire thus exposed the Bulgarian people to a double exploitation.

(a) The Turks deprived the Bulgarians of statehood and all their local organs of government and integrated them as an inferior class in the Ottoman Empire. They levied crushing taxes and on the slightest provocation sent their troops into the countryside to abuse and massacre the population. Their raiding detachments stole young girls in large numbers for the harems of the leading Turks. They recruited by force large numbers of boys for the Corps of Janissaries (1330-1826),[15] a fanatical unit composed entirely of denationalized and Mohammedanized ex-Christians, devoted completely to Islam and its Sultan-Caliph. The Janissaries were a particularly feared and hated corps which, as an élite troop of 100,000 men, won many victories for the Sultan and Islam in the early years of the Turkish expansion. The Turkish terroristic regime forced a growing stream of Bulgarian emigration into all the neighboring countries.

(b) The Greeks, once given the ecclesiastical control of the Balkans, deprived the Bulgarians of their national church, their hierarchy, and so far as possible, their clergy. The Greek bishops who shared the "great Hellenic idea" began to eliminate all traces of Bulgarian culture, the Liturgy, the language, the script, schools and literature. In every field where Bulgarian had been used, Greek began to penetrate. Even the Greek monks on Mount Athos heated their ovens with Slavic manuscripts. They oppressed the Bulgarians culturally and introduced an era of intellectual darkness and ignorance. The Greek bishops sent into Bulgaria were usually the least educated and were ecclesiastical tax-gatherers and businessmen. They entered the villages with Janissary protection to gather the taxes for the Phanar and were interested only in plundering the Bulgarian dioceses. Step by step this process Hellenized the church, the public and commercial life of the country, and the entire system of education. Greek became the medium of communication of all who aspired to any post of prominence, in learning or in business.

This Hellenization met with the most bitter opposition and resistance from the peasantry in the villages, especially those in the mountainous area of the Balkans, and from the artisans and workers of the cities. Thus at the time when Greek seemed to be gaining among the better classes, the Bulgarian language was still used exclusively in the remote villages and in the many small monasteries scattered throughout the mountainous regions.

Here the speech and the traditions remained alive and vital. The Bulgarian peasant, with his spirit of industry, became the decisive force in the struggle for the self-preservation of the Bulgarian nation and proved himself more powerful than the denationalized city man.

However, in the cities, too, the artisans and craftsmen maintained their own culture and did not adopt that of the so-called upper classes. Their guilds, once the Ottoman government was induced to grant them charters, became again a vital force in the Bulgarian movement and acted as centers of intense Bulgarian patriotic and national consciousness. The two forces combined saved the nation from oblivion and extinction.

The situation was most desperate in the field of education. The only schools which existed were the *kiliynaya* schools[16] which were run by semi-literate Greek teachers in connection with the Greek churches in the different cities and villages. It was thus very difficult for a Bulgarian to secure even a limited education and almost impossible to secure any in his native tongue. Few of the students could hope to go to the leading Greek schools like that of Chalki in the Sea of Marmora where some degree of education along religious lines was given. There was some education possible in the Bulgarian monasteries on Mount Athos, the Holy Mount, but even there the system of education, devoted to a study of the monuments of the past, offered little for the needs of the present.

As the Turkish Empire grew weaker, the situation became worse. The Sultans proved themselves unable to control their local and provincial governors who set themselves up as almost independent potentates with the one aim of gouging the last possible sums from the Christian *rayah*.[17] In the 18th century such semi-outlaws as Pazvantoglou, Pasha of Vidin, with their bands, ravaged much of Bulgaria. The Janissaries too became restless and went off to plunder on their own in defiance of the will of the Sultans whom they attempted to make and unmake with disturbing regularity and for little discernible reason.

Yet even under these difficult conditions, it was still possible for unscrupulous Bulgarians to make personal fortunes by playing the Turkish game and exploiting their own people. These were the *chorbadji*,[18] who were as cordially detested by the population as were any of the other oppressors, for they bound the peasants by lending them money at usurious rates, and they added through this their own exactions. Men of this type were not interested in any amelioration of the lot of the the peasants. They were largely in league with the Phanariote agents of the Patriarch and the representatives of the Sultan. This did not save them personally from the exactions of the other oppressors but though they groaned over payments that they were often forced to make, they soon found ways to recoup their fortunes and to continue on their bloodsucking careers. These men, partly Bulgarians and not by any means entirely Hellenized, fought stubbornly against the introduction of any enlightenment or education into occupied Bulgaria, and they were always ready to denounce to the authorities of state and church any individual who incurred their displeasure or jealousy.

Under these circumstances there was the danger that in the course of time the Bulgarian national character would be broken because the country was suffering from devastation, depopulation, and the migration of many of the stronger and more ambitious individuals.

Any Bulgarian resistance or open opposition to this political Turkish and religious Greek oppression and economic exploitation was hopeless during the period of Turkish expansion because of the country's geopolitical position. All the roads leading to the Danube, to Hungary, Austria and Western Europe passed across Bulgarian territory, and therefore Turkish armies in force were constantly moving to and fro across its territory. These were the years when all of Europe and Christendom was confronted with the danger of Turkish conquest and all armed opposition from Europe met with disaster. The period is marked by the Christian defeat at Varna where the Polish King Wladyslaw met his death (1448), Kosovo (1448) where Hunyadi Janos of Hungary was defeated, Mohacs (1526), where the Jagellonian King Louis of Hungary lost his life, and the first siege of Vienna (1529). Although these dates meant much to Europe, Europeans were not aroused to meet the Turkish menace seriously or to try to liberate the Bulgarians and other Christians of the Balkans.

It is true that there were at this period certain emissaries who tried to arouse Europe to the need for Bulgarian liberation. Such were the merchant Pavel Djordjevich (1520) and the great Bulgarian patriot Peter Parchevich, a Bulgarian boyar, who was sent in 1657 by Emperor Ferdinand to Bohdan Khmelnytsky, Hetman of Ukraine, to try to reconcile the Hetman and the Poles so as to induce him to join with Poland and the Empire in an attack upon the Ottoman Empire.[19]

Opposition became a little more feasible after the Turkish Empire was seriously weakened by the crushing of its fleet by Don Juan of Austria at Lepanto (1571) and still more so after the crushing defeat at Vienna (1683) when that capital was saved by the bravery of the Austrians and the Polish King Jan Sobieski. Sobieski, whose title was *Rex Poloniae, Magnus Dux Lituaniae et Ukrainae* (as given on his monument in Vienna), had with him a detachment of Ukrainian Kozaks who were regarded as specialists in fighting the Turks. This battle struck a death blow to Turkish power and produced repercussions in Bulgaria. Thus after Lepanto there was a revolt in Nikopol (1598) and after Vienna, in Tirnovo (1686), in Chiprovets (1688), and in Sofia (1737-1738). In addition to these there was the continuous activity of the *hayduks,* groups of outlaws fighting the Turks on behalf of the Christians. The *hayduks* have lived on in Bulgarian folksongs and traditions.[20]

After the battle of Vienna, the Hapsburgs began to take the offensive against the Turks and the course of events favored the Bulgarian revival. The Austrians liberated Hungary and then crossed the Danube and seized Belgrade. When they gave it back to the Turks, they protected the Orthodox Christians by inviting the Serb Patriarch Arsen Tsrnoyevich with his followers, some 36,000 families, to settle in the military frontier north of the Danube (1690). These Serbs did not receive the full autonomy that they had been promised but the Orthodox Serb centers of Karlovtsi and Novi Sad had an opportunity to develop under Austrian rule, to stimulate anti-Turkish feelings throughout the Balkans, and to become acquainted through Vienna with the progress of Western European thought.

The other factor that favored the Bulgarian revival was the appearance of the Russian Empire on the Balkan scene. This was the result of a long process of development. Tsar Ivan III of Moscow had married the heir to the Paleologue throne in Constantinople and put forward the claim to be the heir of Constantinople with Moscow as the Third Rome. Muscovy grew in power and the tsars extended their claims to be the legitimate rulers of the Eastern Slavs. When Tsar Alexis in 1654 by a treaty with the Ukrainian Kozak Republic concluded an alliance with that state, the tsars regarded it as an act of subordination and by clever manoeuvering finally secured the control of Kiev. Their next move was to transfer almost by force the jurisdiction over the Metropolitanate of Kiev from Constantinople to Moscow and in 1685 to suppress all the liberties and practices of the Kievan Metropolitanate. They also forbade the printing of Ukrainian church books and substituted those printed in Moscow. Then looking southward they flooded the Balkans, both Serbia and Bulgaria, with Russian books. Thus in the 18th century the Balkan Orthodox felt the influence of these works and a Muscovite South Slavic Church language began to exercise considerable influence.

In 1709 Peter I defeated at Poltava Charles XII of Sweden and his Ukrainian ally, the Hetman Ivan Mazepa, gaining the opportunity to change the Tsardom of Muscovy into the Russian Empire. He used the Ukrainian territory that he had thus acquired to spread Russian influence down to the Black Sea and along its coasts in the hope that he could seize Constantinople. Russian control of the Black Sea meant the crushing of the Khan of Crimea, a vassal of the Sultan, and extended Russian influence into the Danubian Principalities. By the Treaty of Kuchuk Kainardji in 1771 Russia forced Turkey to recognize her as the protector of all Orthodox Christians in the Ottoman Empire, thus securing for the Russians the possibility of interfering at will in Turkish affairs. The destruction of Mohammedan influence along the northern and northwestern shores of the Black Sea and the foundation of cities like Odesa offered improved opportunities for trade. The Russian government encouraged the emigration of the Bulgarians and there slowly grew up Bulgarian colonies of merchants in Odesa and other coastal cities. These colonies prospered. The rich Bulgarians who formed them were sharply distinguished in the minds of the people from the *chorbadji*. They had different ideas of patriotism and by the beginning of the nineteenth century these new émigré colonies consisted of men who were able and willing to help their unfortunate brothers in their homeland. The early stages of the Bulgarian revival owe an infinite debt of gratitude to these colonies abroad, for they were of great assistance in developing the Bulgarian spirit as it showed itself in the first half of the nineteenth century.

We can see from this brief review of the past greatness and tragedy of Bulgaria the elements that promoted the development of the Bulgarian national consciousness. Before the end of the first Christian millennium the Orthodox Church and the Church Slavic language had developed for the Bulgarians a common culture, and their struggles for independence from Byzantium fostered in them a Slavic consciousness as opposed to the Greek. The Bulgarians felt themselves at this early period an independent nation. This feeling preserved them during the interregnum between the First and Second Bulgarian Empires. Even after the Turks destroyed the Second Empire, the Bulgarians still retained, despite their humiliation, the consciousness of their separate national character and their separate fate. No matter how confused that consciousness became, it still existed and only awaited a favorable moment to reassert itself.

The fact that this spirit was already in existence made it possible for modern Bulgarian nationalism to create on a historical basis an idealized image of the fate of the Bulgarian nation in the past and to place at the center of the conception of their national culture the "sacred ideas" of the contribution of the Bulgarian saints and tsars to the whole of Slavic Orthodox Christianity and culture and then to project a concept of Bulgaria's mission in the future in terms of the past. These ideas and ideals were summed up in the greater idea of the beloved "motherland" so as to inspire dynamic patriotism and rouse the people for the struggle for the resurrection of the Bulgarian tsardom. It was an idea that was forged through centuries of struggles and conflicts with their neighbors, especially the Greeks and the Greek Orthodox Patriarchate, struggles that gave the Bulgarian revival many of its distinguishing features.

All of these ideas were reflected in the culture and literature to which we shall turn in the following chapters.

CHAPTER TWO

Old and Middle Bulgarian Literature

To appreciate and understand the writings of the early leaders of the Bulgarian revival in the eighteenth century, we must glance back at the work of the earlier periods, even though many of these books had largely passed out of the conscious memory of the people and were preserved in a small number of copies only in some of the monasteries in Bulgaria proper or in those of the neighboring countries. Yet they had left confused memories which soon took proper shape, once the intellectual interests of the people were turned in that direction.

As we have seen, there are practically no remains of the Altaic-speaking Bulgarians. Their few remaining monuments, such as the Krum Monument at Madara, mostly contain inscriptions in broken Greek. It was not until the time of SS. Cyril and Methodius that there existed anything that we can call a Bulgarian literature. There was the folklore but even here the Altaic and Slavic sources were thoroughly amalgamated.

SS. Cyril and Methodius were widely travelled and highly educated men and in preparation for their work in Great Moravia, they had prepared some translations. They wrote these out in a very unusual script prepared by Cyril-Constantine, the so-called *Glagolitsa*.[1] This was apparently heavily influenced by some of the scripts of Asia Minor and the Caucasus, for it shows more similarity to these than to the Greek minuscule from which it has been often derived. After their deaths, a new and more readable script came into use, the so-called *Kirilitsa* (Cyril's script), although it is fairly certain that it developed later than the *Glagolitsa* either in Okhrida or Preslav. This is based frankly on the Greek majuscule with the addition of certain letters that were necessary to express sounds which existed in Slavic but not in Greek. It very soon displaced the *Glagolitsa* in the eastern part of the Balkans and is now the basis of the alphabets of all the Slavic Orthodox or Uniat peoples, the Bulgarians, Serbs, Cossacks, Russians, Ukrainians, and Belorussians. It was once used even for Romanian and Albanian. The *Glagolitsa* steadily withdrew to the west to Okhrida and Athos, where it was used until the end of the twelfth century, finding its final home in some of the Croatian monasteries on the Dalmatian coast.

It is worthwhile mentioning that there is a story that connects the origin of the *Glagolitsa* with the present Ukrainian city of Kherson. Constantine was sent on a mission to the Khazar state (860-861) on the lower Volga and on his way he disembarked at Kherson to travel overland. The *Life of Cyril* says of this:

> "And he found there a copy of the Gospel and the Psalms written in Ruce characters (*ros'sky pismeny pisano,* variant *rous'sky*) and he found a man speaking this language and spoke to him and understood the meaning of what he said, and, adjusting it to his own dialect, he analyzed the characters, both the vowels and the consonants, and praying to God, started quickly to read and speak (the Ruce language)."[2]

Whether the story of the script is to be accepted historically is not yet certain but at all events Constantine in Kherson came into direct contact with the ancestors of the modern Ukrainians who were already speaking in that area the original form of their present language.

It is fair to presume that SS. Cyril and Methodius employed as the basis for their translations from the Greek the language of the Slavs around Salonika, the Macedonian dialect which they had spoken since childhood, although in Moravia they added words and phrases that were of local origin there. In spite of the fact that some Macedonians consider themselves today a separate Slavic nation with its own language, the Bulgarians stoutly maintain that the language which many scholars call Old Church Slavic is really Old Bulgarian. Even though it was written outside of Bulgarian territory, in the narrower sense of the word, it was used, developed fully and flourished on Bulgarian territory.

The Christianization of the Bulgarians created the demand for (a) an Orthodox "ritual" literature on the one hand and (b) a "didactic" literature or literature of instruction on the other, to strengthen and deepen the Christian world outlook and ideals. These religious needs had to be satisfied by translations from the Greek, a circumstance which stimulated the Bulgarians to produce some original works. Let us briefly survey the more important works of the old and medieval periods.

St. Cyril commenced his work with the translation of the Service Books of the Church, the Liturgy of St. Chrysostom, and the necessary passages from the Gospels and Epistles. It is also possible that he translated part of the Old Testament. We are still more certain that he put into Old Bulgarian the *Nomocanon,* the Church regulations, and the *Paterik,* a collection of short lives of the saints. Among the original writings of this period is the *Life of St. Cyril,* apparently by his brother Methodius, and the *Life of Methodius,* which is usually assigned to the latter's pupil, St. Clement of Okhrida (d. 910). Both *Lives* underscore the approval of the Slavic Liturgy by the Apostolic See in Rome.

The work of the two brothers was continued by their disciples, St. Clement, Bishop Konstantin, and Ioan the Exarch. Working at Okhrida, the center of Macedonia, and at Preslav, the capital of Bulgaria, under tsars Boris and Simeon, these men and other unknown translators put into the language of the Bulgarians other selected translations mostly from Greek religious texts and writings. Later they began to use this material more or less independently to create an Old Bulgarian ecclesiastical literature.

The most novel work of this period was undoubtedly that of the Monk Khrabar, *On Letters* (the Slavic Characters). We know nothing of the life or other works of this monk but he left a very original, polemical and patriotic defense of the action of St. Cyril in forming a Slavic alphabet. He boldly claims that it is superior to Hebrew, Greek or Latin, because it was made in a few years and at one time by a Christian saint.

The apology is one of the most curious documents of this period and shows the Slavic antagonism to Greek cultural domination and claims.

When we sum up the achievements of Bulgarian literature in these first Christian centuries, which included the so-called "Golden Age" under the rule of Tsar Simeon (893-927), we find them rather impressive. The most important translations in the different fields are: in the Christian "ritual" literature, the Gospel (Tetraevangel) with its beautiful images and comparisons, its majestic language and moral content which established the standards for literary values; the Bible, completed by Gregory the Presbyter, which functioned as a kind of encyclopedia for the time; the Apostle, including the Acts of the Apostles and the Epistles; and the Psalter, with its heartfelt lyricism. These were the favorite reading of the period.

In theology, which was the cornerstone of medieval culture, the basic manual of the Orthodox Christian doctrine was *The Exact Exposition of the Orthodox Faith* by St. John of Damascus, translated by Ioan, Exarch of Bulgaria. Among the other works were: *Treatises* of Athanasius of Alexandria and Gregory Nazianzen; *Commentaries* on the Gospel by Presbyter Konstantin; *Commentaries* on the Psalter, the Psalms and the Prophets; collections of *Sermons* which explained the whole system of the Christian faith; and the *Menea* for reading, with its large gallery of Christian heroes and saints, often told in novelesque form, often fantastic and usually thrilling. Very popular was the *Zlatostruy* (Golden River), a collection of excerpts from the sermons of St. Chrysostom and Epiphanius of Cyprus. For the Old Testament there was a condensation of the *Paleia*. We must also mention the *Revelations of Methodius of Patara,* the Sybilline books of Byzantium.

Among the translations in the field of history were the *Chronographia;* the *Chronicle* of Malalas; the *Chronicon* of Georgius Monachus (Hamartolos), starting with Adam and Eve and finishing with the death of Emperor Theophilus (842), with some general information on Plato and the work of Georgius Synkellus. But there were surely other books by Bulgarian chroniclers which have not survived.

In the natural sciences we have the *Hexaemeron* (the Six Days of Creation), edited by Ioan, Exarch of Bulgaria (with short notes on the teachings of Plato and Aristotle); a commentary on *Genesis;* and the *Physiologus,* a medieval compendium of natural history, with fantastic stories about the self-sacrifice of the pelican, the phoenix rising from the ashes, the unicorn, and other animals, plants and minerals.

In the field of jurisprudence there were compiled in Bulgaria *The Court Law for the People* and the *Nomocanon.*

In the sphere of *belles-lettres,* the Church eagerly sponsored didactic novels. This genre is represented by some of the classic themes of world literature and includes the legendary biography of Alexander the Great, a most popular, fantastic novel which developed in the second and third centuries A.D. in the cultural sphere of Alexandria, Egypt, and was included in the *Chronicle* of Malalas; the *History of Troy* which was also included in the *Chronicle* of Malalas; the "ideological" novel of *Stefanit and Ikhnilat* which has been traced back to India in the fifth century and then reached Bulgaria by way of Persia, Arabia and Byzantium; *Varlaam and Josaphat,* the history of Buddha, which originated in India in the sixth century B.C. and was Christianized in Byzantium and then transmitted to Bulgaria; the story of *Akir the Wise,* based upon a Hebrew story in the *Book of Tobit* (second or third century B.C.) with its moral "Whoso digs a pit for another to fall into, will fall into it himself"; and the *Deeds of Digenis,* an epic of the Greek frontiersmen in Anatolia defending Christianity against Islam (a later translation).

It is probable that the East Slavic apocryphal *Story of Solomon and Kitovras* (Centaur), which appears as one theme in the legend of Merlin, is also from Bulgaria.

A good example of the secular literature can be seen in the *Collection* (Izbornik) of Svyatoslav, which was originally compiled for the Bulgarian tsar but preserved in Ruce-Ukraine. It consists of an abridged collection of aphorisms, historical and philosophical treatises, theological expositions and lists of the Roman and Byzantine rulers.

Other popular works of literature were the *Apocrypha.* These books were not sanctioned by the Church as parts of Orthodox religious literature but they included such pieces as the *Gospels* of Nicodemus, Jacob and Thomas and many others, "supplementing" the Old and New Testaments with stories about various persons and events mentioned in the Bible and Church history. The themes of some of these entered into Dante's *Divina Commedia*, the works of Milton, Klopstock and Rilke, and even supplied the prototype for the Grand Inquisitor in Dostoyevsky's *Brothers Karamazov.*

The great wealth of themes and the wide dissemination of the *Apocrypha* are due to the fact that the official religious Church literature, with its theological definitions and subtleties, could not satisfy the mind and soul of the masses. They raised countless questions of "human interest" on such matters as the life of our Lord and His Mother, Adam and Eve, the history of the tree from which the Holy Cross had been made, the Apostles, patriarchs and martyrs, Satan the archenemy of Christ, hell and paradise, the creation and destruction of the world. The *Apocrypha* answered this curiosity and thirst for knowledge with a vast quantity of "true stories," the marvels of which were limited only by the imagination of the narrators. They fascinated and astounded the readers. This apocryphal literature became very popular among the peasants, whose agricultural work was warmly honored and blessed by another apocryphal book purporting to be by Christ Himself. From Bulgaria these *Apocrypha* wandered to all Southern and Eastern Slav nations and even to the Western Slavs. They absorbed similar western *Apocrypha* from Latin and German sources which were in the sixteenth century even published in Cyrillic by the Franciscans in Bosnia. Finally in the Slavic countries these developed into a flourishing prose-epos which influenced the folklore and stimulated the development of drama. Much of this literature cannot be dated and among the Southern Slavs and in Ukraine it maintained its popularity into the beginning of the nineteenth century.[3]

This apocryphal literature which was as a rule translated from Byzantine sources was greatly stimulated by the Bogomil movement which developed in Bulgaria in the tenth century.

The feudal state and church, both organized on the Byzantine hierarchical principles with the current pomposity of the time, disappointed and confused the believers and created a kind of scepticism. The Bogomil doctrine must be regarded as a protest and resistance against the Byzantine forms of state and church organization and an attempt to seek for individual salvation through a moral perfection ostensibly on the basis of the Gospel and by the liberation of mind and soul from every state and church authority. The dissatisfaction of many good Christians with the existing state of affairs was again intensified by the schism in the Universal Church (1054) and the ensuing struggle between the Eastern and Western Churches.

An interesting figure of this period was the Priest Kozma who died in 969. He is known by his one sermon against the new Bogomil heresy.[4] This gives in some detail a picture of Bulgarian church life of the day, by no means flattering, for he mercilessly criticizes the haughtiness and worldliness of both the bishops and the monks, features that were all too common in both the East and the West. He also tells much of the teachings of the Bogomils and their peculiar doctrines and social philosophy which, despite an anti-ecclesiastical and anti-governmental trend, were very popular among the poor and oppressed peasantry, for they offered an explanation of the real origin of social inequality. Yet with all his merits, Kozma represented a point of view that was to become dominant in the next centuries, a profound conviction that the truth had already been entirely revealed and that all problems would be resolved if people lived up to the obligations imposed upon them by tradition.

On the other side there was undoubtedly a large amount of Bogomil literature and many legends which were later suppressed and destroyed, for the Bogomils and their leader, a priest, Jeremiah, were skillful mythmakers and their ideas easily penetrated many of the apocryphal legends and colored them, as they spread throughout the Slavic Orthodox world. Yet again we notice that these ideas largely were in the religious field, and the secular life of the population passed almost unnoticed by both the Orthodox and the heretical sects. Religion was the dominant interest. We have few accounts of the secular and state leaders except when they were deemed worthy of sainthood and their lives could be handled within the framework of hagiography.

These tendencies lasted into the Second Bulgarian Empire, which produced even less literature than did the first. It was the period when Hesychasm (a form of quietism) and mysticism swept the entire East and Bulgaria followed again in the path of Constantinople. However, in the fourteenth century the country did develop some interesting writers such as Patriarch Evthimi (Euthymius), the author of several *Lives,* especially one of St. Ioan Rilski, the founder of the Rilo Monastery and patron of Bulgaria (died 946). Evthimi established a school in Tirnovo with some fifty students and this made Tirnovo a Slavic Athens for the Southern and Eastern Slavs.

His student and admirer, Grigory Tsamblak, continued his work. He left Bulgaria after the Turkish conquest of his country and tried in vain to be recognized as the Orthodox Metropolitan of Kiev, after that ancient Metropolitan see had been practically abandoned by its holders, who had transferred their seat to the rising Moscow. Tsamblak, who was well known and supported by Ukraine, was for a while even at the Council of Constance in 1418. He failed in his endeavors and finally died in a monastery in Moldavia. Among his chief literary works was a *Sermon* in praise of Evthimi. Another pupil of Evthimi, Yoasaf, wrote a moving description of the *Downfall of the Capital of Tirnovo.*

We have now reached the most disastrous event in Bulgarian history, the conquest of the country by the Turks and the suppression of all Bulgarian independent institutions.

At that period with the ever increasing menace of the Turks, the Bulgarians and the Serbs began to cooperate more closely. Thus Konstantin Kostenetski, the philosopher, wrote a biography of Knez Lazar, the Serb leader who was killed at Kosovo and became a symbol of joint Slavic resistance to the Turks. In this quite unusual work, although it is written in Serb, Konstantin, a pupil of Evthimi, wrote a really secular biography without the usual hagiographical details and embellishments. In fact, it was almost the first distinguished secular writing that was done by an educated Bulgarian.

All of these writers had been afraid of introducing into their works the purely vernacular forms which in the course of time had developed in Bulgarian and separated it from the norms of the Old Church Slavic. They had tried to accept and preserve the old traditions of Bulgarian as these had been worked out by SS. Cyril and Methodius and their disciples some centuries earlier. Yet almost against their will they failed to maintain the purity of the old language and with the fall of education which came during the Turkish invasion, it became more and more impossible for the authors even to pretend to do so. The number of persons literate in Bulgarian even among the clergy steadily declined as the Greek influence grew greater and greater.

Thus for centuries the chief books that were available for those persons who knew how to read were the so-called *Damascenes*. These were in their original form the Greek works of Damascene the Studite and consisted of pious stories and moral examples. There were several translations into Bulgarian and, almost against their will, the translators introduced words, phrases and constructions from the vernacular so as to make the books intelligible to their readers. This was the first step in the formation of the modern language but it was still a literature that was frankly looking backward to the traditional genres of religion and theology, although these subjects were treated superficially.

The people, deprived of close contact with educated leaders and groaning under the pressure that was exerted upon them from all sides, cherished perhaps even more carefully their popular folklore and especially folksongs. These had undoubtedly existed for centuries in oral tradition and therefore followed the popular speech. The older clergy had frowned upon them and such men as Kosma could see little difference between them and the Bogomil productions since both were the work of the devil, i.e., not the products of the Church and the Church culture. The folklore was the creative self-expression of especially talented persons or the collective creations of social groups in the pure Bulgarian vernacular and it constituted for the peasant class a real "people's" literature; it was handed down orally from generation to generation in an unbroken but ever changing stream from the primitive Slavic times and represented the living literary and historical archives of the nation. This folklore included the whole life cycle of the family with all its joys and sorrows, the various stages of the peasant cycle of the year, the ritual songs connected with birth, weddings and funerals, other ceremonial songs, and also fairy tales, proverbs and pagan magical formulas. By the end of the eighteenth century, the value and beauty of these folksongs and of the folklore in general were becoming recognized by European scholars and the efforts to collect and preserve the oral tradition of the various peoples spread into the Balkans. Consequently large numbers of folk-creations were finally preserved from the lips of native singers before they perished under the impact of the modern world.

The most striking of these songs are those dealing with King Marko, the lord of Prilep, who also figures as one of the chief heroes in the Serb heroic epos. Both the Serb and Bulgarian songs are written in the same ten-syllable metre and they are very similar in spirit. Marko, the son of King Vukashin who fell in the battle on the Maritsa River in 1371, was an historical figure of the period of the Turkish conquest. It is very difficult to understand why he should have been singled out for special consideration. He took no part in the battle of Kosovo, although the Serbs have tried to bring him into some connection with it, and he seems to have died fighting in the Turkish ranks in 1393. He was apparently a stormy and reckless fighter, perpetually at odds with all his neighbors. He had difficulties with his wife who left him for the arms of another princelet, Mina of Kostur. He may have been of tremendous physical strength, for that is how he appears in both the Serb and Bulgarian versions of his exploits, although the Bulgarian poems seem to be far closer to life and more realistic than do the Serb legends which idealize his character.

Yet, whatever the reason, he is presented as an ideal figure and a true champion of the oppressed Christians. As a kind of Balkan Robin Hood, he rescues the innocent, he frees them

from Turkish prisons, and inflicts tremendous punishments upon the Turks for their inhuman persecutions; he does not hesitate to beard the Sultan even in his own palace in Constantinople
when need arises. The feats of Marko cover a period of a
couple of centuries and several sultans, although we know that
the real Marko died at a relatively early age.

Marko became the true paladin of the Bulgarians and the
Balkan Slavs in their dark hours. His friends and co-fighters
include the traditional heroes of all the peoples who were drawn
under the Turkish yoke, and behind them we can recognize
such persons as the Transylvanian Hungarian Hunyadi Janos
or the Romanian Yanko of Sibiu and representatives of nearly
all the non-Greek peoples of the Balkans. Apparently they all
needed an ideal, a hero, and, for whatever reason, their choice
fell upon Marko, who became the immortal hero of the folk
epos on a tremendous scale. We can see in him the glorified
exponent of a unified Balkan Orthodox Slavic culture as it was
forged by the struggles of more than five hundred years.

Closely associated in spirit with the Marko tradition are the
hayduk songs of later origin. Marko carries us back to a period
when there was a living consciousness of Bulgarian national
independence and a national state. They reflect the glories of
the past. The *hayduk* songs are different for the *hayduks* were
the outlaws of the Balkans. They were men who had suffered
unjustly at the hands of the Turks and who, instead of yielding
passively, had gone into the mountains and forests and there
in small guerilla bands, had waited for the opportunity to take
summary vengeance upon their oppressors and enemies. These
enemies included not only the Turks themselves and their
agents but also the *chorbadji,* the rich Bulgarians who had made
their peace with the invaders and were profiting in their service
and recouping any personal losses that they might incur from
the Turkish regime by grinding down still further their unfortunate fellow-Bulgarians. In this sense the *hayduk* songs have a
strong sense of social justice and stimulated popular revolt
against the upper classes. They are similar to those songs in all
countries where popular discontent born of unjust treatment
by those who should have been the people's protectors glorifies.

the outlaw who steals from the rich to reward the poor and also opposes an unjust foreign regime. These songs were especially popular among the Ukrainians, the Slovaks and the Poles along the Carpathian Mountains where the forests furnished a refuge for freedom and justice. We can well look at the *hayduk* songs as the precursors of the modern national movement in Bulgaria and link them with the ideas of men like Botev who threw themselves definitely into the arms of modern radicalism and the class struggle.

Thus during the Turkish occupation and the Greek cultural domination, the national spirit of Bulgaria took refuge in her folklore. It returned to the very springs of the Bulgarian national consciousness, finding shelter in the creative forces of those classes which had preserved the Bulgarian traditions most fully, the peasants and the craftsmen.

Yet the preceding centuries of Bulgarian Christian literature represent not only glorious pages in the history of Bulgaria itself but they are of far-reaching importance for the whole Slavic world including Croatia and Serbia and especially the Eastern Slavs. The Belo-Ruthenians and Muscovites received their faith from Kiev, the old capital of Ruce-Ukraine and the center of Slavic Christianity for all eastern Europe. However, this Ruce-Ukrainian center of Kiev, with its celebrated Lavra Monastery, received its Slavic Christianity and the Slavic script, along with the fairly diverse types of translated literature and the Church language and even the first Church hierarchy, from the Patriarch of Okhrida perhaps more than from Byzantium. This Church language, which originated in Bulgaria, for a couple of centuries was also the "holy language" of the churches in Moldavia and Wallachia (Romania) and Albania which were at that time integrated in this sphere of Slavic culture.

The importance of old Bulgaria and its literature for the whole Slavic world is well expressed by one of the great Slavicists, V. Jagić,[5] in these words:

"The ancient Bulgarian literature had attained such a phenomenal development in the number of books of a church and religious character that it was able to accumulate, that it may justly take its rank side by side with the richest literatures of those days, viz. the Greek and Latin. It certainly surpassed all the other European literatures of the same kind. Strictly speaking, during those times, Church literature existed in only three languages: Greek, Latin and Slavic."

Summing up, we may say that this old Bulgarian literature and the period of Bulgarian history in which it was produced are of fundamental importance to the whole of Slavdom. Bulgaria succeeded in maintaining and preserving the achievements of the Slavic apostles and educators in Great Moravia; it gave the Slavs a Slavic Church language for divine services which soon became the Slavic literary language of the time; it presented to the Slavs a rather impressive literature and thus laid the basis for Slavic education and culture. Bulgaria is the cradle of Slavic civilization. From the earliest times this Bulgarian-Slavic Christianity was marked by a deep emotional consciousness of race and nationality, as we can see from this panegyric of St. Cyril by his disciple Clement in the tenth century:

"By the grace of Jesus Christ, thou didst come among men as shepherd and teacher, and like a lion, thou didst open thy mouth against the three-language monopoly of the heretics who, blinded by envy, preached that it was derogatory to praise God in any other language except Hebrew, Latin and Greek, and out of malice became the accomplices of Pilate. Thou didst destroy their blasphemies with plain parables. Having translated the rubric from the Greek into Slavic, thou wentest to Rome."[6]

This national religious world outlook was backed by such personalities as Tsar Simeon who had the ambition to consolidate Slavdom in the Balkans not only in the religious sphere but also politically.

The Turks and Greeks, jointly, nearly annihilated those *Bulgarian social classes in the church, the court, and the state* which were the creators and bearers of the old Bulgarian nation and its literature and which in previous centuries, as the intellectual and political élite, had assured their historical continuity. During the period of Bulgaria's decline and fall, the clergy in the face of the Turkish menace tried to keep the hope of resurrection alive by developing the myth that their Bulgarian Tirnovo was destined after the fall of the Second Rome, Constantinople, to become the Third Rome of Christianity. As the plight of the Bulgarian Church became worse with every decade and the once famous monasteries became dependent upon the gifts of the rulers of fellow Orthodox nations, especially of distant Moscow, the clever Bulgarian monks changed the Tirnovo of the myth to Moscow in order to justify their visits there and to increase the generosity of the Muscovite Church and Court. Thus the Bulgarian Church, after the fall of the nation, implanted in Moscow the myth of "Moscow, the Third Rome" in the early sixteenth century. This doctrine, proclaimed by Filotey,[7] became the basis of modern Muscovite-Russian imperialism and in fact contributed to the final disintegration of the Ottoman Empire and the liberation of Bulgaria.

Earlier still, the Bulgarian ecclesiastical diplomats, apparently looking for an ally against Byzantium, sought the aid of the dynasty of Ruce-Ukraine by spreading the *Legend about the Babylonian Empire,* the imperial crown and insignia of which were "brought" to Byzantium and from there "transferred" to the dynasty of Volodymyr. With the decline of Kiev and the rise of Muscovite-Russian imperialism, this legend also landed finally in Moscow for its "glorification." It found there favorable soil not only as a result of the Mongol tradition but it was later reinforced by another stimulus from the western territory of the Southern Slavs. There clashes with the Italians also developed an ardent Slavic nationalism and induced the Dominican Juraj Krizhanich, the Father of Pan-Slavism (1618-1683), to visit Moscow for the propagation of the idea of a Slavic Empire under the leadership of Moscow. Although he was imprisoned in Siberia by the Moscow Tsar for fifteen years till he escaped, his political ideology was to be put to good use in the service of Muscovite expansion.

The eighteenth century seemed to be a period when the forces of oppression in Bulgaria were at their zenith. The culture of

CHAPTER THREE

Father Paisi Khilandarski

As was so often the case in the revival of the Slavic nations during the eighteenth and early nineteenth centuries, the initiative was given by a book which reflected in a more or less conscious form the long suppressed aspirations of an oppressed nation and was written in a form and language which could be understood by the common people and not in the traditional mode of expression.

Such a work for the Bulgarians was the *Istoriya slaveno-bolgarskaya o narode i o tsarey[1] i o svetikh bolgarskikh i o v'sekh dyeyaniya i bitiya bolgarskaya—The Slaveno-Bulgarian History about the Nation, the Tsars and the Bulgarian Saints and All the Acts and Life of the Bulgarians.* The title-page then adds: "Collected and Arranged by Paisi, a Hieromonk who was in and came to the Holy Mount Athos from the Diocese of Samokov in 1745 and prepared this *History* in the year 1762 for the use of the Bulgarian Race."

The title page of the manuscript tells us almost all that we know about the author, who is, at best, a shadowy but powerful figure in the Bulgarian revival, and about the scope of the work and the purpose for which it was written. We can learn a few other details from some allusions in the work itself and a few notes which have survived of his activities but otherwise the life and career of Father Paisi are still veiled in an impenetrable mystery.

His secular name has nowhere been preserved. However, he seems to have been born in 1722 in the diocese of Samokov which included the celebrated Monastery of St. Ioan of Rilo, the most important monastery in western Bulgaria. He seems to have been educated in a typical *kiliynaya* school where he probably learned some Greek and little else, for he laments that he had learned "neither grammar nor politics." He may have spent some time at the Rilo Monastery but in 1745 he went to Mount Athos and became a monk in the Monastery of Khilandar (Chilandar), where his brother Lavrenti had already preceded him.

Mount Athos, the Holy Mountain,[2] was the center of Orthodox monasticism and of Orthodox learning at the time. It is a mountainous tip of the Peninsula of Chalcidice, almost cut off from the mainland on the north shore of the Aegean Sea and is renowned for its rugged scenery. Athos has had a remarkable history. In pre-Christian times it was a sanctuary of Zeus. Greek medieval tradition identified it with the "high mountain" on which Satan tempted Christ. Near it at Philippi St. Paul first preached on European soil. In the fourth and fifth centuries it was already the home of individual hermits and by the ninth century a monastic organization had taken shape. The Byzantine Emperors granted autonomy to the monasteries and, like the later rulers of Orthodox countries, were benefactors and protectors of this monastic republic which served also as a refuge and place of retirement for statesmen and rulers who had wearied of their secular posts or been thrown from power and had sought shelter in monasticism.

The republic consisted of twenty fortified monasteries. Among them were the famous Greek Lavra, the Serbo-Bulgarian Khilandar (Chilandar) and Zographu and that of St. Panteleymon, and the Rossikon for the monks of the East Slavic peoples. The monasteries of this "Holy Land" had libraries, art collections and unique archives of Classical, Greek and Slavic manuscripts. The Latin Crusaders after the capture of Constantinople (1204) treated the monks rather brutally; they appealed to Pope Innocent III and he took them under his protection but the monks later remained stoutly Orthodox. In the fourteenth century Athos was the center of Hesychasm, which even in the sixteenth century produced such a remarkable representative in Ukraine as Ivan Vyshensky (1550-1621). Because of the voluntary submission of Athos to Sultan Murad II even before the capture of Constantinople, the Turks respected its autonomy and granted to this territory (which no woman was permitted to enter) the unique privilege in the Ottoman Empire of ringing church bells. In the eighteenth century the Academy of the Vatropedi Monastery was, for a time, a center of Greek learning. By tradition a common council of the leading monks ruled this territory and made all arrangements with the Sultan. Yet, despite this cooperation on the material plane, the monasteries had an ardent national consciousness. The monks disputed among themselves on many questions of national pride and political tendencies and the repercussions of these discussions were felt far outside Athos.

The founder of the Monastery of Khilandar was reputed to have been the first Serb ruler, Stefan Nemanya, who retired to it and died in the year 1200. His son, the Patron of Serbia, St. Sava, also lived there during much of his eventful life. Yet through the centuries and especially after the Turkish conquest it was filled with both Serbian and Bulgarian monks.

Father Paisi, who had accepted monasticism there, used the opportunity to study among the rich collection of manuscripts that existed on the Holy Mount, apparently taking part in the frequent national disputes. He says himself that he was mortified to find that the Bulgarian monks had no records of the past of their nation. They were mocked in the discussions as mere peasants, shepherds and workmen and he decided to do something about it.

In 1761 he was sent with a letter of recommendation to Karlovtsi in the Austrian dominions to receive for his monastery a bequest which had been left to it by the Karlovtsi Archbishop and Metropolitan Pavel Nenadovich. He was, according to this letter a prohegumen and a man of especial loyalty and zeal. He signed for the property May 21, 1761. His stay at Karlovtsi was very fruitful, for there he apparently became acquainted with the historical works of Mauro Orbini (died in Ragusa, 1614, *Regno delli Slavi,* 1601) and of Caesar Baronius (Cardinal and librarian of the Vatican, 1538-1607), two historians who had written in Italian or Latin histories of the Slavs which had later been translated into Russian.

At Mount Athos he could acquaint himself with the works of all the leading Byzantine historians and follow in detail the fortunes of the First and Second Bulgarian Empires. He speaks of Bulgarian histories, the *Kormchaya Book,* "Ruce and Muscovite printed histories," a German history, Serbian books, *Prologues, Lives of the Fathers, Admonitions of the Fathers,* and imperial *chrysobouli* (the so-called "golden bulls"). Thus we have evidence that he was more or less familiar with the chief available sources for Bulgarian history.

On his return to Mount Athos from Karlovtsi, he found the monks of Khilandar quarreling over a payment demanded by the Sultan. Paisi, unwilling to be involved and concerned with his great work, transferred to the Monastery of Zographu and in 1762, despite ill health, finished the work.

Apparently he had no intention of allowing his manuscript to be buried in the archives of Mount Athos or any of its monasteries, for in 1765 he had the manuscript in Kotel where a young priest, Stoyko Vladislavov (later Bishop Sofroni), made a copy of it. We find another copy of the manuscript prepared in the diocese of Samokov, his native locale. In 1784 he met a Serbian archimandrite, Gerasim Zelich, in the city of Kareya, where he acted as interpreter in discussions with the Greeks and admitted that he hated the Greeks. This is the last reference to Father Paisi as a living man but apparently, after wandering around Bulgaria and leaving copies of his manuscript behind him, he returned to the Monastery of Zographu where he died at an unknown date late in the century. His manuscript was not printed until a revised version appeared in Budapest in 1844 and even then his name was not connected with it until it was republished by the revolutionist Georgi Sava Rakovski in 1869. At the present time about forty copies and revisions are known to exist. This speaks volumes for the energy with which Father Paisi carried out his self-appointed task of spreading a knowledge of their past before the Bulgarians of the eighteenth century.

Father Paisi was not an objective historian in any sense of the word. He wrote for the patriotic purpose of making the Bulgarians conscious and proud of their past and he does not hesitate to express his personal feelings about Bulgaria's neighbors. His chief antipathy was for the Greeks who had used their imperial position in the past to wipe out the First Bulgarian Empire and who had profited by the Turkish conquest of Byzantium and the fall of the Second Bulgarian Empire to impose their will upon the Bulgarian nation and to humiliate it psychologically, materially and ecclesiastically. Yet he does not hesitate to give his opinions about the Serbs whom he charges with misrepresenting the Bulgarians, although the latter had long controlled the Serbs. He attacks their early rulers for having been Latins. He condemns their Emperor Stefan Dushan (1333-1355) for his crimes and for having proclaimed himself tsar and for having worked against the Bulgarians. He likewise does not spare the Ruce (Ukrainians) and the Muscovites for boasting that they were the first Slavs to accept Christianity, although they had no proof of it. (This is apparently an allusion to the legend that St. Andrew the Apostle had preached on the site of Kiev.) Yet he is more restrained in his comments about the Ruce and Muscovites.

Admitting that the Serbs in Austria and the Russians of his day had better education and were more enlightened than the Bulgarians, he attributes this to the fact that they had their national independence and church freedom which had given them opportunities to study. The Bulgarians, because of the Turkish political yoke and the Greek ecclesiastical control, lacked such opportunities. He also saw rightly that the reason for this was the relative nearness of the Bulgarians to the capital of Constantinople.

In his discussion of the Ruce-Ukrainians and the Muscovites, there is a certain ambiguity. His use of old books showed him clearly the difference between the two nations. At the same time the newer help which was coming from St. Petersburg used the one word, "Russian," and we may doubt whether he understood fully or even cared to understand the political events in eastern Europe during the seventeenth and eighteenth centuries.

Paisi was not trying to write a history of the Slavs. He wanted to revivify the Bulgarians and he chose the best possible means for doing it under the conditions of the time, when illiteracy was nearly universal and political and cultural suppression was the order of the day. Aiming to adapt his style and subject matter to the needs of the moment, he produced a work which was eminently readable, if not altogether objective and historical.

His language shows the same purpose. He wanted to write in the language of the people but there was little agreement regarding the forms that language would take. There was no written Bulgarian contemporary language except that which aped the language of the Church services. That was obviously archaic and unsuited for his purposes. At the same time, as a literate man, he had had to familiarize himself with the Serb and Russian writers and their varying styles. As a result the language of Paisi shows a groping for a written Bulgarian and it is easy to pick out phrases and expressions that have not stood the test of time or passed into the present colloquial or written speech.

All this does not detract from the fact that Father Paisi, a humble monk of Mount Athos, had conceived the grand idea of restoring the Bulgarian nation to its past greatness by re-vivifying its consciousness of its historical continuity and linking it with its great past. To the best of his ability he cut through the stories of the recent past and raised a standard to which forward-looking Bulgarians could rally. His work was epoch-making and while he could not foresee the course of events in the near future, he did something that was extraordinary for his own time. He wrote and distributed a history that restored in ever increasing measure the Bulgarian self-respect and set into motion the revival of the Bulgarian nation. He included in their mental sphere possibilities for the future instead of dwelling only on the traditions of the past. In so doing he became the inspirer of modern Bulgaria and the father of modern Bulgarian literature. Moreover, from the very beginning, as the title *Slaveno-Bulgarian History* shows, Father Paisi was aware that the Bulgarians belonged to Slavdom, to the culture of which Bulgaria had contributed so much and in defense of which Bulgaria had fallen victim to the Greeks and the Turks.

In evaluating the work of Father Paisi Khilandarski, the first herald of the Bulgarian revival, we must not overlook some links connecting him with the previous period. The *Damascenes* of Joseph Bradati mentioned such subjects as the nation, the language, and Greek bondage but they spoke of these with an attitude of Christian resignation and without any active will to resist and fight. There were also some Bulgarian church books that had been printed as the *Psalter* (1562) and the *Prayer Book* (1570) by Yako Kraikof of Sofia in Venice and the *Abagor Prayerbook* (1641) of the Bulgarian Paulicians. There were two Bulgarian schools in Sofia in the sixteenth century and a theological seminary existed in the seventeenth century in the town of Chiprovets. We must not overlook the work of these earlier Bulgarians, but they did not include in their objects the reawakening of the Bulgarian national spirit.

That was the purpose of Paisi's *History*. His work was a protest against and a blow to the imperial designs of the Greek Patriarchate in Constantinople with its dreams of the complete Hellenization of the Balkans.

Paisi became the ideologist of the Bulgarian Renaissance and he clearly outlined its tasks, which were to bring about, through the revival of the Bulgarian National Church and the Bulgarian school, the revival of the Bulgarian State. Paisi was a fighter and he stirred the conscience of his fellow Bulgarians with his scathing rebuke:

> "O thou foolish and degenerate man, why art thou ashamed to call thyself a Bulgarian? Have not the Bulgarians had a Kingdom and Empire of their own? Why shouldest thou, O imprudent man, be ashamed of thy nation and shouldest labor in a foreign tongue?"

By this and similar remarks, Paisi kindled the sense of Bulgarian self-assertion and self-respect and these qualities expanded in the revived Bulgarian nationalism.

CHAPTER FOUR

Educators and Revolutionists

The seed sown by Father Paisi was very slow in germinating. It could not well be otherwise for his work circulated in only a few manuscript copies among an illiterate people. Those who were able to read, almost to a man preferred to read Greek, which was the language used by the Church and by the dominant Christians in the Ottoman Empire. As a result we find few reactions to Father Paisi's work during the next decades among the Hellenized leaders of the country.

In the meantime the Turkish dynamism was exhausted and that fact was being recognized abroad. Even at the height of their power, the Turks had been unable to conquer the Slavic Christians living in Montenegro, the rugged area around Mount Lovchen in the western part of the Balkan Peninsula, and this state under the heroic leadership of its Prince-Bishops remained a symbol of liberty through the entire Turkish period. It became an example and ideal for all victims of the Turkish oppression and thus a herald of the disintegration of the Ottoman Empire.

Meanwhile the pashas and the janissaries continued their unruly course. In 1804 they massacred a number of the leading Serbs and drove the *rayah,* the Christian peasants, to armed revolt. The peasants chose as their leader one Karageorge, a man who had been associated with the *hayduk* activities among the Serbs. To the surprise of all he proved himself a capable military leader. In a few years he set up an independent Serbian government in Belgrade. It is true that the Turks soon overwhelmed him and drove him into Hungary but it was not long before a more modest movement under Milosh Obrenovich secured for their leader recognition as the Supreme Prince of a small but autonomous state of Serbia.

In the same period the young Greeks who had been educated abroad returned with a consciousness of the events in America[1] and of the French Revolution and the Napoleonic struggle. They formed their own secret societies and soon the Turks became aware of the Greek danger to the Empire. When the Turks on March 25, 1821 (Annunciation Day), hung a number of Greek bishops, the Greeks rose in revolt. After years of struggle, publicized in Western Europe by the death of Lord Byron at Missolonghi in 1825, the Greeks succeeded in enlisting foreign aid. Soon after the allied fleets of Great Britain and Russia destroyed the Turkish-Egyptian fleet at Navarino (1827), Greece entered the ranks of the European nations (1828). The Greek revolutionary movement was supported by some Hellenized Bulgarians and groups of Bulgarian patriots like Hadji Khristo with his cavalry and Hadji Stephcho with a body of infantry. One Bulgarian, Marko Bodjar, became a legendary hero among the Greeks under the name of Marko Bozzari.

These events could not fail to affect the Bulgarians. It encouraged many of the wealthier Bulgarians to renew their efforts to secure a Greek education and thus to some degree postponed the Bulgarian action which was sooner or later inevitable as the influence of Father Paisi's work spread from the monks and clergy to the lay population. The class that was most responsive in a way was that of the Bulgarian emigrants: the Bulgarian merchants in the Danubian principalities, Moldavia and Wallachia, the later Romania, and in the Bulgarian colonies along the north shore of the Black Sea in the Russian Empire. These émigrés could not fail to become aware, through their daily contacts, of the ideas of the French Revolution and the movements that were agitating the whole of Europe. It was these merchants who began to send money home to establish schools in their own communities which tended to stress the use of the Bulgarian language rather than Greek.

The first and most ardent disciple of Father Paisi was the young priest Stoyko Vladislavov (later to be Bishop Sofroni Vrachanski, of Vratsa). He was born in 1739 in the city of Kotel in northeastern Bulgaria and he became a priest in 1762, the year when the *History* was completed. It was only three years later when he secured a copy from Father Paisi, although we have no knowledge of the circumstances and no account of the meeting of the two men. Stoyko was impressed and to the end of his life he fought valiantly for the ideals expressed in the *History*. His life was one long martyrdom for he was constantly harried by the Turks and persecuted by the Greek hierarchy and the rich *chorbadji* who objected to his work for his poor compatriots. In 1794 he was consecrated Bishop of Vratsa, a poor and ruined diocese. Here he had no peace. He was forced to flee from one place of refuge to another and even for a time found shelter in a harem. He finally gave up the uneven struggle and in 1800 he went to Vidin on the Danube where he served as bishop for three years. Then in 1803 he succeeded in crossing the Danube and went to Bucharest where his grandsons were living. Here he was treated kindly by the Metropolitan and here he died in 1818. His last years were filled with efforts to secure Russian assistance for his people. In 1804 he sent two friends to St. Petersburg with letters from him attempting to interest Tsar Alexander I in the Bulgarian cause, but without results.

He wrote copiously on religious subjects and one of his books, a *Nedyelnik* or *Sermons* for every Sunday in the year, came out in 1806 as the first printed book in modern Bulgarian. His main work was his autobiography, *The Life and Sufferings of the Sinful Sofroni*. It gives a vivid picture of the man and is the first book in Bulgarian to picture conditions in the country through the eyes of a Bulgarian. With no pretensions to literary style, Sofroni wrote in the simple Bulgarian of his day. Like Paisi he regretted and stated that he did not know the Church Slavic well enough to write it. Yet he was one of the first clergy to introduce into the services in his diocese Church Slavic instead of Greek and to use the books which had been sent by the Russian tsars.

The impulse to the use of Bulgarian given by Father Paisi and Bishop Sofroni soon began to affect the laity. During the first half of the nineteenth century the leaders of the Bulgarian revival were lay educators who sought to make up for the long lag in Bulgarian education. The first of these men was Dr. Petar Beron who was born in 1793 also in Kotel where his wealthy father had built at his own expense the first school building in the Bulgarian lands. His father lost his money during the Russian-Turkish War and the young Petar went to Bucharest to study in a school kept by a Greek named Vardalachos. Petar supported himself by giving private lessons. In 1821 he went to Brashov in Transylvania as a private teacher for the children of a successful Bulgarian merchant, Anton Yovanovich. Beron prepared his own textbooks and Yovanovich published for him in 1824 a Bulgarian dictionary, the first of its kind, called the *Fish Dictionary* because of a fish on the cover. Yovanovich later sent Beron to Germany where he was graduated as a Doctor of Medicine in 1832. He returned to Bucharest. He soon gave up medicine for business and was so successful that in 1842 he practically retired and went to Paris to study the mathematical and physical sciences. In 1871 he returned to Romania for his last visit and there he was brutally murdered on his estate. He left all of his money for educational work in his native city of Kotel and in Odrin.

Beron was the best-educated Bulgarian of his day and his activities had much to do with the introduction of lay schools into the country. His dictionary was the first to appear and in it as in all his writings he used the spoken Bulgarian of the time. He was also the first to object to corporal punishment in the schools and to advocate schools for girls. While he was not a devotee of *belles-lettres,* he laid the groundwork by his philosophical, educational and scientific works for the men who were to come after and undertake the art of writing for its own sake.

Another of these wealthy Bulgarian émigrés who did a great deal for the cause of education not only by the giving of money but by participation in the work was Vasil Aprilov. He was born in 1789 in Gabrovo, a small city fifty miles south of Tirnovo. His father died when he was ten years old and his brothers who were in business in Moscow took him there and placed him in a Greek family so that he could perfect himself in that language. Later he went with them to Brashov, Vienna and Constantinople but when he grew older he went to Odesa and started business there in 1811. In the next years he was an ardent Hellenophile and zealously supported the Greek struggle for independence. For a while he was a leader of the Greeks in Nizhyn in Ukraine, the city where Gogol (Hohol) attended school.

Then in 1829 and 1830 he read the books of Yury Venelin,[2] the most devoted friend of the Bulgarians at the time. Aprilov read his books attentively, corresponded with Venelin and soon became fired with the Bulgarian possibilities. Aprilov then threw himself wholeheartedly into the Bulgarian cause and in 1835 persuaded some of his associates in Odesa to join him in financing a school in his native city of Gabrovo. This became the first modern school in Bulgaria. Aprilov sought out the best-prepared teachers and the success of the school led to the opening of similar institutions in other parts of the Bulgarian lands.

Aprilov not only contributed funds but he took an active part in writing and publishing books for his school. He stoutly defended the theory that the original language of SS. Cyril and Methodius was Bulgarian and not either Serb or Russian. He was a strict purist and protested against the introduction of Hellenisms into the modern language and also against the Russianisms which had been brought in through the Church Slavic books sent by the tsars to Bulgaria. Finally, following the example of the day, he published in 1841 the first collection of Bulgarian folksongs.

He was bitterly opposed to any revolutionary movement in Bulgaria but he sought instead to improve the condition of the Bulgarians within the Ottoman Empire. In his view this goal required the creation of an independent Bulgarian Orthodox Church. Therefore, he became a leader in the ecclesiastical struggle against the Patriarch which raged throughout the middle of the century. He died in 1847, the first of the great benefactors of Bulgarian education.

Beron and Aprilov were both relatively rich men who worked abroad for the good of their people and tried to revive the

Bulgarian cultural tradition by engrafting on it the achieve-ments of Western Europe and Russia. They stoutly defended the Bulgarian language but neither knew by personal experi-ence the difficulties of work within the country. In this respect they differed sharply from Neofit Rilski (of Rilo), a devout monk, who was at the same time the best teacher in Bulgaria with a broad practical experience of work in the field.

Neofit, whose name as a layman was Nikola pope Petrov Benin,[3] was born in Bansko about 1793, where his father was a village priest. Despite his father's objections he became a monk in the Rilo Monastery and secured his education in the Greek schools in various places. He was first assigned as teacher in Samokov but most of his life was associated with the Rilo Monastery. Thanks to the influence of Aprilov, he was sent to study in Bucharest and when the Gabrovo school was opened, he was appointed one of the teachers and was often consulted by residents of other communities who wished to open modern schools. He disagreed on several points with Aprilov and finally left Gabrovo and continued his teaching in various other cities, in the Rilo Monastery, and finally in the Greek school on the island of Chalki in the sea of Marmora, the fore-most Orthodox institution of the day in the Ottoman Empire. He soon left there and returned to Rilo where he died in 1881.

His nephews were in the service of Prince Milosh of Serbia and it was through them that he was able to publish his Bul-garian grammar in 1835 in Kraguyevats, Serbia. This was the most successful grammar of the time. It attracted considerable attention and proved a successful adjunct to his teaching. Despite some peculiarities and a tendency to rely upon the language of the Russian Church books, he was moderate in his position and was counted the foremost teacher of the day. He also translated the New Testament into Bulgarian for the British and Ameri-can Bible Societies. Neofit Rilski was wholly absorbed in his work, and it was largely due to him that so much progress was made in a relatively short time.

He had little interest in things other than education. His only appearance outside of school work was on a mission to Constantinople to secure permission for the rebuilding of the church in the Rilo Monastery which had burned in 1833. He succeeded in this and the Rilo church was the first important building to be erected in Bulgaria in centuries. His career as a peaceful educator was markedly unlike that of Neofit Bozveli who was constantly engaged in a bitter struggle against the Greeks.

Neofit Bozveli was born in Kotel in 1783 and received his early education from Stoyko Vladislavov (not yet Bishop Sofroni). Then he became a monk in the Monastery of Khilandar. In 1814 he was sent to the city of Svishtov where he remained for a quarter of a century as a priest and teacher. Yet his wider interests constantly drove him to interfere in public life and involved him in constant difficulties with the Greeks. In 1811, he published the first of his two dialogues, *An Enlightened European*. Later, in 1835, he published in Serbia a series of Bulgarian textbooks and then in 1844 his second dialogue, *Mother Bulgaria.*

He paid dearly for his efforts to erect a Bulgarian Church in Constantinople. The Bulgarians tried to have him made Bishop of Tirnovo but failed. Nevertheless he was sent there in a minor capacity and engaged for years in bitter disputes with the Greek bishop. He was imprisoned in a Greek monastery on Athos for some years. He escaped and resumed the struggle and then was consecrated bishop by the Patriarch and kept by him in his official dwelling, the Phanar. He ran away and again was captured and imprisoned on the Holy Mountain where he died in 1848.

His dialogues have real literary value despite their character as political tracts. In the first he pictures Mother Bulgaria as a desolate hermit in a cave on the River Yantra near Tirnovo with her half-dead son who bewails bitterly the suffering of his people. This is so great and so inhuman that the Enlightened European (from whom the dialogue takes its name) cannot believe in its reality.

The second dialogue, *Mother Bulgaria,* is even more eloquent. Here Mother Bulgaria appeals to her son to know why things are as they are. The son laments his inability to tell the whole story:

"I should need the heavens for paper, the seas for ink and the years of Methusaleh and summon forth from the poems of the God-inspired Tsar, the prophet David, the marvellous Homer, the admirable Vergil, the magical Ovid and the laments for Jerusalem of the prophet Jeremiah so that I could bring alive this death-dealing woe and definitely show you, Mother, that conditions are like those of Jeremiah and you may see with him and learn sadly and piteously to mourn your children. They have lips and speak not, they have eyes and see not, they have ears and hear not, they endure more than the animals and why they do not dare to ask."

He continues with impassioned eloquence to denounce the *chorbadji*, the Turks and the still more evil Greeks who were working in an underhanded way along with the Turks and poisoning all the thoughts of the people. He rises to real eloquence in his denunciations and his ardent national feeling turns a political pamphlet into genuine literature.

Neofit Bozveli was the last of the militant ecclesiastics and monks who played an outstanding role in the Bulgarian revival. By his day the movement had passed fully into the hands of the laity and the possibility of a secular struggle for independence or education had become so good that ambitious young men chose lay occupations rather than the limitations of a clerical career. The succession that had started with Father Paisi had now changed its shape and Neofit Bozveli was on the dividing line.

The emphasis that these early men placed on education developed into a powerful movement for it appealed to the Bulgarian thirst for learning, an outstanding feature of the Bulgarian character. After the foundation of the school at Gabrovo the movement spread rapidly and by the time that Bulgaria won its independence there were 1,892 Bulgarian schools (some 300 in Macedonia). This number was more than in Greece (1,468 schools in 1878) and Serbia (565 schools in 1885). The Bulgarians established three gymnasia (Bolgrad in Bessarabia, Gabrovo and Plovdiv). The young men then attended the Universities in Athens (where there was a Bulgarian Student

Association), Austria, Germany and especially Russia. These far-flung institutions became very popular because the Russian government, as well as the wealthy Bulgarian colonies, gave many scholarships to Bulgarian students. In this connection it was important that the Bulgarian students usually stayed in the south in Ukrainian territory between Odesa, Nizhyn, Kiev and Kharkiv. They were brought into contact with the renaissance in Ukrainian literature and the rising Ukrainian nationalism which offered many analogies to their own efforts.

The educational movement was supported by the peasantry, which recovered economically after the Turkish reforms of 1839, and by the guilds. It was supplemented by the Reading Room Associations (started in 1856), the Sunday Schools and the Women's Associations (after 1856). These were mostly led by the patriotic village schoolteachers who through their Teachers' Conferences took charge of the movement. Even some of the *chorbadji* began to found schools. This widespread effort has much in common with the development of the American system of education, based upon the efforts of the communities as a whole.

During these decades, too, the number of printing presses multiplied both within and outside of Bulgaria. The presses at Salonika, Bolgrad, Belgrade, Bucharest, Vienna, Smyrna and Constantinople owe a great deal to the American Bible Society. In all between 1806 and 1875, despite the obstacles, the Bulgarians published at home and abroad some 800 books to fill the various needs of the nation. They also started a large number of newspapers, although many had but a short life, especially in the early days.

The first Bulgarian newspaper was the work of Konstantin Fotinov (1800-1858). He spent the bulk of his adult life in Smyrna, Asia Minor, where he published in 1842 the first Bulgarian periodical *Lyubosloviye* (Love of the Word). This appeared more or less regularly and contained information of all kinds on Bulgaria and its past. It was printed on the same press that was used by the British Bible Society for the publication of a Bulgarian translation of the Bible. Fotinov himself worked

on the Old Testament. The journal lasted only two years because of financial difficulties.

Fotinov's work was continued by Ivan Bogorov (1818-1892)
who published the *Bulgarian Eagle* in Leipzig in 1845. He
later transferred his activity to Constantinople where he achieved
even more with his *Constantinople News* (Tsaregradski Vestnik,
1848-1861). This publication touched all subjects except politics, a topic too risky in the political situation of the time.
Shortly before the Russian-Turkish War of 1877 Bogorov returned to Bulgaria and continued his activity there. He was
often criticized by his compatriots for his theories, but his
papers distributed much useful information to the people. His
work found increasing respect after his death, when it was
considered in the light of history.

These "enlighteners" believed in evolution rather than revolution. They sharply dissociated their activities from those
movements which aimed to disintegrate the Turkish Empire
and the most that they did was to agitate for the creation of
an independent Bulgarian Church within the Ottoman Empire,
something that they finally obtained in 1872. Yet we must not
underestimate their work. They changed the face of Bulgarian
society, tore its culture away from the antiquated Greek models
and Greek education and oriented it on the pattern of Odesa,
Kiev, and Western Europe, especially Germany. They gave the
Bulgarians pride in their past and confidence for the future.
Naturally, at the present time in Communist Bulgaria their
efforts are treated with disdain. Nevertheless, they had much
to do with turning the amorphous mass known to Father Paisi
and Bishop Sofroni into a people which, however crudely,
were able to administer after liberation their own governmental
institutions and to provide the nation's political leaders for
the next period.

The work of implanting dreams of political independence
and of fighting for independence was not done by these men
but by their opponents, the revolutionists, who objected to the
limitations of their policy and called for armed revolt. The
revolutionists all too often cast away their lives in futile gestures

but they attracted the attention of the European countries, especially Russia. They were imbued with the spirit of the old *hayduks* even though, in many cases, they had received some education and political knowledge and were guided by more than the spirit of elemental revolt.

In a sense the oldest and perhaps the most typical of this group was Georgi Sava Rakovski who was born in 1821 in Kotel. Several of his uncles had distinguished themselves in the Russian-Turkish War of 1827 and had suffered for their Russophile sympathies at the hands of the Turks. After some preliminary education in his home city, Georgi was sent to Constantinople in 1837 and there in a Greek school he secured a good knowledge of Modern and Classical Greek, French and Latin. He joined a Macedonian Society formed by patriotic Bulgarians to plan a Macedonian uprising to coincide with a Greek revolt in Crete and Thessaly. The plan failed and Rakovski took refuge in Braila in 1841. His plotting there was exposed and the police finally caught him and sentenced him to death. Still, as he had a Greek passport, they consulted the Greek consulate, which sent him to Constantinople. Here the Greek Minister sent him secretly to Marseilles instead of to Athens. From France he returned to Kotel where he and his father were seized on the complaints of some envious *chorbadji*. The two were taken to Constantinople and held for three years in a Turkish prison. When Rakovski was released, he worked for a time as a lawyer in Constantinople and cooperated with Bogorov on the journal. The outbreak of the Crimean War roused him again to action and he joined the Turkish army with the intention of acting as a spy for the Russians. Next he found himself in Kotel and from there he escaped to Romania. In 1856 he was in Novi Sad, a Serb city under Austrian rule, where he edited a Serb journal, *The Bulgarian Morning Star*. This activity involved him in trouble with the Austrian authorities and so he made his way to Odesa in 1858. By 1860 he was in Belgrade trying to form a Bulgarian legion to fight for Bulgaria in the Serb army. However, when Belgrade was freed of a Turkish garrison, the Serbs lost interest in the fight for the liberation of the Bulgarians and Rakovski went to

Romania. He collected *hayduk* forces there but before they could cross into Bulgaria and start fighting, he died in Bucharest of tuberculosis in 1867.

We have gone into some detail about Rakovski's life and activities because he was typical of the older circle of revolutionists who attempted to combine simultaneously with revolution some aspects of the work of the enlighteners. Rakovski wrote several poems such as *The Herald* and *The Mountain Wanderer*. In the latter work he describes a *hayduk* with his twelve followers drawn from different parts of Bulgaria. Each of them tells of the special hardships from which his own people are suffering. Then the leader talks with three old Bulgarians and, with a warning to his men to be heroic and fight for the liberation of their country, he leads them off into the mountains. Rakovski was in no sense a great poet but his songs struck the imagination and the hearts of his people. Thousands of young Bulgarians learned by heart *The Mountain Wanderer*, which inspired them for the struggle ahead.

In addition Rakovski edited various Bulgarian journals in which he published historical documents that came into his hands; he wrote copiously on ethnology and folklore and did not fail to add to them many philological articles in which he pictured the Bulgarian language as the source of almost all others, often with a grotesque misinterpretation of known facts. Yet all his works had the object of making the Bulgarians conscious of their past and of raising their national morale for the coming military conflict with the Turks and the campaign against the Greeks so as to secure from the Porte the foundation of an independent Bulgarian Church.

Rakovski was a combination of *hayduk* and literary man. He was not typical either of the *hayduks* or of the mass of the writers who defended the cause of independence. The writers' weapon was usually the pen. Such was Nayden Gerov (1821-1900) from Koprivshtitsa who during his long career as a teacher, Russian consul in Plovdiv and then as a scholar after the liberation worked steadily and almost exclusively in the literary field. He finally published the first large Bulgarian dictionary and many valuable articles on Bulgarian history. He is perhaps more important in literature as the first modern Bulgarian poet. While he was studying in Odesa at the Richelieu Lycée in 1841 he wrote to his former teacher Neofit Rilski:

> "I have some fables and Bacchic songs and other works written in poetry. When they are finished, I shall publish them. I have used the tonic measures like the Russians."

He enclosed a translation of Krylov's fable, *The Eagle,*[4] *the Crab and the Pike*. His range of subjects was limited to love songs and revolutionary poems which did not appear in print. In 1845 he published a longer poem, *Stoyan and Rada,* a romantic melancholy tale of two lovers in which the boy's mother will not give her consent to the marriage he desires but forces him into a marriage with a girl whom he does not love. The wedding never takes place for as the procession nears the church, Rada falls dead and Stoyan dies in despair on her body. It is a typical romantic tale and in some details reminds us not only of the general Slavic romanticism of the time but of prose stories like that of Kvitka-Osnovyanenko,[5] *Marusia,* which was of about the same period (1833).

What Nayden Gerov did not succeed in accomplishing was brought into being by Petko Rachev Slaveykov, the foremost Bulgarian poet of the mid-century and one of Bulgaria's outstanding writers. Slaveykov was born in Tirnovo in 1827. His father, Racho Kazandjiyata, was very poor but he gave his son as good an education as he could in the Greek and *kiliynaya* schools. The boy's education, however, ended when he was sixteen. He at first thought of becoming a monk but his father advised against it and in 1842 let his son read a manuscript of Father Paisi. The boy then commenced to teach school in Tirnovo. At this time he wrote a satire in which he lampooned the Greek metropolitan. When the poem came to that dignitary's attention, Slaveykov was forced to flee. In the next years he taught all over Bulgaria, never able to remain long in any one place because of the hostility of the Turks and of the Greek hierarchy. During these years he continued to write verses but they were crude and undeveloped. Yet all the time he was learning to master the poetic art, and his natural gifts were ripening and developing. For a while he taught in Trevna, where he married. His troubles began again and he was forced to continue his wanderings.

In 1852 he published in Bucharest three volumes of poems: a translation of Aesop's *Fables, A Mixed Bouquet* (Smesna Kitka), and a third volume of songs, satires, etc. to amuse the readers. In 1846 he had been given a copy of Galakhov's *Russian Chrestomathy* and during the next years he used this zealously and not only familiarized himself with the devices of Russian poetry but made translations from Krylov, Pushkin and Lermontov. In 1855, through the influence of the Bulgarians in Odesa, the Russian Academy of Sciences published a volume of his *Bulgarian Songs.*

Slaveykov's poems are filled with a pensive romanticism. At the same time he had a keen sense of realism and of the beauties of nature. As a result he introduced into Bulgarian literature for the first time an appreciation of the beauties of the Bulgarian landscape. His love of his native land led him to glorify the national past, and at one time he thought seriously of undertaking a long poem and incorporating into it the folksongs about King Marko. He gradually extended, chiefly through Russian translations, his knowledge of the western writers, especially Goethe, and he put his knowledge to good use. His poems show his love and feeling for life even in his frequent satirical and ironic vein. It is to be noted that only later did he come to know the Ukrainian poet Taras Shevchenko,[6] and in his last years he made several free translations from Shevchenko's poems for they appealed to his sense of national devotion and idealistic realism.

His *Calendars* for 1857 and 1861 were especially interesting. In these he provided for every day in the year some pithy saying which condemned the vices he saw in the Bulgarian life around him. At the same time he did not spare the oppressors of his own people. Later he prepared still other calendars but they were not so biting or successful as his earlier attempts. Thus as he matured in his art, he maintained that same unflinching idealism and patriotism that grew out of his Christian view of life.

In 1864 Dr. Albert Long, a Protestant missionary in Bulgaria, induced Petko Slaveykov to go to Constantinople to work on a Bulgarian translation of the Bible which was to be published by the American Bible Society. He devoted himself to this task for several years and meanwhile took an active part in the struggle for the foundation of an independent Bulgarian Orthodox Church. In 1874 he was forced to leave Constantinople, and after a short stay in Odrin he went to Stara Zagora. During the Russian-Turkish War his house was burned, and he lost many of his manuscripts, including unpublished works and his large collection of folksongs. This was the worst tragedy of his life. After the liberation he continued to teach and write with still more maturity and freedom until his death in 1895.

Throughout his long career Slaveykov constantly remained in touch with the Bulgarian people. His strong sense of reality kept him from indulging in ventures that did not answer the needs of the moment. He showed equally in his satires, his lyrics and his two journals, *Hayda* and *Macedonia,* which he published in Constantinople, his understanding of the feelings of his people. He remained to the end of his life one of their respected leaders in the fight for freedom and democracy. Literally a home-grown product, though his style in later times seemed a little primitive to some of the more educated writers, we can say truthfully that he was in a real sense the first poet and man of letters to appear in modern Bulgaria, and many of his poems have not yet lost their charm.

Of the other writers who were born about the same time as Slaveykov we must mention especially the two brothers Miladinov, Dimitar (1820-1862) and Konstantin (1830-1862), from Struga in Macedonia in the neighborhood of Lake Okhrida. Both men were teachers and both passed some time abroad, one in Austria and the other in Russia. Their great work was the publication of a large collection of Bulgarian folksongs which they succeeded in publishing with the aid of Bishop Josef Strossmayer,[7] the great Roman Catholic Bishop of Zagreb who took a lively interest in all the various Slavic peoples. The book was scarcely published when it was learned that Dimitar had been arrested and thrown into a Turkish prison in Constantinople. Konstantin returned to that city but he had barely arrived when he, too, was thrown into prison also on false charges. After a few months the two brothers died from the ill treatment which they had received. Their work remains as a monument to their industry and zeal.

Although the struggle for an independent Church produced a great deal of literature, some of it with literary value, the outstanding man who was born in the thirties is undoubtedly Lyuben Karavelov, who first introduced into Bulgarian thinking the ideas of the Russian radical thinkers of the sixties. Karavelov was born in 1837 in Koprivshtitsa. After receiving his early education there, he went to Plovdiv and entered the Greek gymnasium. He was repelled by the crudities of the city and the evil life that he saw around him. He stubbornly refused to enter business, as his father desired, and instead secured a position for a while in Constantinople. After the Crimean War he decided to go to Russia. In 1857 he passed through Odesa on his way to Moscow. There he soon fell under the influence and adopted the ideas of the Russian leaders of the sixties, the radical intelligentsia such as Herzen, Chernyshevsky, Dobrolyubov and Pisarev. He was for a while a free auditor in the University of Moscow, and he there became acquainted with many of the Slavophile leaders such as Ivan S. Aksakov who encouraged him to study the culture of other Slavic peoples. He was no less attracted to the new Ukrainian literature. He read the stories of N. V. Gogol (Hohol) and the poems of Taras Shevchenko, but he was also especially attracted to the stories of a younger Ukrainian authoress, Marko Vovchok,[8] who pictured the hardships of the Ukrainian women under serfdom. These Ukrainian poems and stories had a special appeal for Karavelov for they showed him that the Ukrainians in the Russian Empire were suffering in the same way as the Bulgarians had suffered under the Turks. It was under the influence of these Ukrainian writers that he began to write his stories of Bulgarian life.

In 1861 he published in Moscow his first volume, written in Russian, *Monuments of the National Life of the Bulgarians.* He included in his book a series of 3,000 proverbs and legends and compared them with those of the other Slavic peoples. He showed his sympathy with some aspects of the Slavophile theories and in fact received 175 rubles toward the publication from Aksakov. However, he did not share the Slavophile political view. He next published in Russian in 1868 *Pages from the Book of the Sufferings of the Bulgarian Race,* including some of his best stories, such as *The Turkish Pasha* and *Bulgarians of the Old Time,* in which the influence of Marko Vovchok is very evident.

Karavelov shared sincerely the ideas of the Russian *Narodniki,* or Populists, those thinkers who based all their hopes for a better social order on the peasants and tried to fit themselves into the peasant mode of life. Led into close contact with the revolutionary movement in Russia, after the attack by Karakozov on the life of Tsar Alexander II, he found it impossible to stay longer in the country, and in 1867 he went to Serbia.

Relations between the Serbs and Bulgarians had cooled since the liberation of Belgrade, but Karavelov tried to apply the new ideas which he had absorbed in Russia and to revive the old sense of cooperation. He wrote copiously on literature and social ideas for the journal *Zastava* (The Banner). His radical views soon made it expedient for him to leave Belgrade for Novi Sad in 1868. Here he became the friend of the leading Serbian writers Svetozar Miletich and Zmay Yovan Yovanovich, and he even commenced an historical novel in Serbian. Written under the influence of Chernyshevsky and Herzen, this novel assailed the reactionary features of Serbian life and the failure to provide for the education and proper training of girls and women. He had an enormous influence on the young, but the critics did not take kindly to him. After the murder of Prince Michael Obrenovich, Karavelov was arrested on suspicion of being involved and was sent to Budapest where he was held for seven months. When he was released, he was hailed by both the Serbs and the Bulgarians as a national martyr. This strengthened his idea that he could unite the two peoples, an idea he held to the end of his life.

Karavelov next transferred his activity to Bucharest. Here he became associated with the Bulgarian National Committee, which was cooperating with the Romanians. This cooperation again became less close after Romania secured its independence. Taking over much of the responsibility for the publication of the journal *Svoboda* (Freedom) and later of *Nezavisimost* (Independence), Karavelov energetically set to work to prepare a general uprising in Bulgaria by founding revolutionary committees in the various towns and regions of the country. He accepted the views of Rakovski as to the way of preparing a revolt and worked strenuously, if not always practically, with Vasil Levski and the other *hayduk* leaders. He was joined in this work by Khristo Botev, who was eleven years younger, but as time went on, and especially after Levski had been betrayed into the hands of the Turks and executed, Karavelov apparently began to doubt whether the path of armed revolution would help the Bulgarians as much as an increased emphasis upon cultural work. He was gradually forced from the position of head of the committee by Botev, who took his place. With the outbreak of the April Rebellion in 1876, Karavelov, more or less discredited by his former friends and associates, retired to Belgrade. With the Russian-Turkish War, his old ardor flamed up. He entered Bulgaria with the Russian troops and made his way to his birthplace, Koprivshtitsa. He soon went to Tirnovo and then to Ruse where he continued his educational work and edited the journal *Znaniye* (Knowledge) and there he died in 1879.

Karavelov held a unique position in Bulgarian life. He was the first to spread in the Balkans the ideas of the Russian *Narodniki* and the revolutionists of the sixties. Yet his plans for a federation of all the Balkan Slavs are perhaps reminiscent of the ideas of Shevchenko and of the Ukrainian historian Mykola Kostomariv[9] in the Society of the United Slavs and the Brotherhood of SS. Cyril and Methodius. Karavelov's ideas certainly differ as sharply from the concepts of organization held by the Narodniki as they do from the Slavophile idea of the position of Russia in any organization of the Slavs.

Karavelov was more of a writer on political and social themes than a man of *belles-lettres,* but his prose stories from Bulgarian life which reflect his own experiences are perhaps the first really successful pieces of imaginative prose in the language. He used these stories to stress his own ideas on the need for human brotherhood and the abolition of human inequality and oppression. He was the most impressive figure of the time, although his fame was much eclipsed by that of his one-time friend Botev.

The first Bulgarian drama was written and produced by a man of Karavelov's generation, Dobri Voynikov. Voynikov was born in 1833 in Shumen, a Turkish garrison town, and educated there. While he was at school, the Turks moved in about 2,000 Polish and Hungarian émigrés who had fought in the Hungarian War for Independence under Kossuth in 1849. The émigrés stayed in Shumen for about a year. They gave the local population a new conception of life in Europe through their entertainments and social life. This had a great effect upon the young Dobri. He was then sent to a French school at Bebek-Constantinople, but his stay there was cut short in two years by the death of his benefactor. He returned to Shumen as a teacher, but he soon aroused the enmity of the *chorbadji* and was forced to leave. He next became a teacher in a Bulgarian school in Braila across the Danube, where he edited a journal *Bulgarska Zora* (The Bulgarian Dawn) from 1867 to 1870. It was while he was teaching in Braila that he conceived the idea of introducing dramatic performances for the entire community, young and old. On January 29, 1866 he presented with local actors his own play, *Voyvoda Stoyan,* for the benefit of the school. Its success was so great that in April he prepared another play *Princess Rayna,* to collect funds for the famine victims in Moldavia. This was performed not only in Braila but also in Bucharest and Galatz. He followed this with comedies such as *The Crooked Civilization.* Voynikov explained that his object was to cultivate the sense of beauty and of virtue in his audiences. For this reason he preferred the historical drama as a means of showing the great examples of the past and the comedy of manners as a vehicle for holding up to ridicule the vices and corruption of his own day. From this point of view his plays served their purpose, even though they are very weak by modern dramatic standards. After the liberation Voynikov was assigned as a teacher in a girl's school in Ruse. He was then transferred to be in charge of an orphan asylum near Tirnovo, but he died of typhus in 1878.

His work as a dramatist was continued by Vasil Drumev who was also from Shumen and born in 1841, apparently of a family of Albanian origin. Drumev became a teacher but in 1858 received a scholarship through the Bulgarian community in Odesa to study in the Odesa Orthodox Seminary. He had already published in Constantinople some translations and an original story, *The Unfortunate Family,* which he had planned while yet in Shumen. All was going well, when he heard of Rakovski's Legion in Belgrade. He dropped his studies and went to Belgrade to join up, but he soon had trouble with Rakovski. When the Legion broke up, he returned to Odesa and succeeded in securing readmission to the Seminary. In 1865 he completed the course and was then admitted to the Kiev Ecclesiastical Academy where a number of anti-Russian Ukrainians were studying. While he was a student in Kiev he completed the drama, *Ivanku,* based on an episode in the Second Bulgarian Empire. In 1869 he returned to Shumen but soon went to Braila where he practically took charge of the affairs of a publishing company which issued a periodical and printed many historical documents like the *Autobiography* of Sofroni. He also became a teacher in the Bulgarian school in Braila. With the establishment of the Bulgarian Church, he was chosen bishop under the name Kliment Branitski. After the liberation he became Metropolitan of Tirnovo. Here he was involved in the troubles caused by the forced abdication of Prince Alexander I of Battenberg and the anti-Russian policy of Stambolov. These political complications were finally cleared up, but he was removed from a seat in the Bulgarian Holy Synod. He died in 1901.

His dramas such as *The Unfortunate Family* and *Scholars and Benefactors* were somewhat artificial, but they contained very effective scenes, even if these were not too well connected and were poorly motivated. On the other hand like Voynikov, he drew, in *Ivanku,* vivid contrasts between the Asens, especially Petar and the Pretender Ivanku, and he aimed to give various pictures of the way in which the Byzantine influence was exerted to create discords in the Bulgarian state. The play was fairly successful.

During this pre-liberation period the Bulgarian national movement had won its main success in the ecclesiastical field, for it secured the creation of an autonomous Bulgarian Orthodox Church. The Bulgarian patriots had fought for this against Greek opposition for forty years in their efforts to retain full control of the Bulgarian dioceses. When they secured from the Pope the right to establish a Bulgarian Church, Russia urged the Sultan to grant Bulgaria in a *firman* (a Sultan's order) a Bulgarian Orthodox Exarchate to have jurisdiction over the fifteen Bulgarian dioceses. The Sultan did this on February 28, 1870, but when the Exarch was elected and appeared in Constantinople in 1872, he and his followers, i.e., the entire Bulgarian Orthodox Church, were excommunicated by the Patriarch. This excommunication was not practically recognized either by the Russian or Serbian Churches and was accepted only by the Orthodox Church of Greece. The result was that the Bulgarian Church finally resumed the control of its own affairs despite the remonstrances of the Patriarch and was able from then on to play its role in the Bulgarian revival, and the note of Greek ecclesiastical tyranny more or less disappeared as a leading theme in literature.

At the same time the writers of the pre-liberation period were steadily improving. They were forging a literary language, they were broadening the themes that they treated, and they were improving their handling of these themes. Many of them were still stumbling, but on the very eve of the liberation a real master put in an appearance. That man was Khristo Botev, who dominated Bulgarian life and literature from his first appearance upon the scene.

CHAPTER FIVE

Khristo Botev

Khristo Botev was the dominant figure in Bulgarian life and thought during the years immediately preceding the liberation. He was the first Bulgarian poet of undisputed literary talent and his twenty-two short poems are almost all among the classics of Bulgarian literature. As a man he was equally striking. He was a colorful figure in the Bulgarian struggle for independence; his heroic death on a desolate Balkan hilltop in 1876 made him a real martyr in the eyes of his fellow countrymen and assured him immortality.

Botev was born on Christmas Day, 1848, in the village of Kalofer in the foothills of the Stara Planina. He grew up in the shadow of the mountains with their living tradition of the brave deeds and adventurous life of the *hayduks*. From his earliest youth he could see the difference between the majesty and freedom of the mountains and of the men who dared to live in them and the miserable lives of the downtrodden population of the villages. His father was a village teacher who had studied in Odesa and was a leader not only in education but in all community affairs. His mother, too, seems to have been an outstanding woman with a large repertoire of folksongs. In this atmosphere the boy completed the three classes of the gymnasium in Kalofer.

When he was fifteen, his father sent him to Odesa where he studied in a gymnasium for two years. He was desperately poor and could not afford even the school uniform. In his first year he was successful in his studies but apparently lost interest, and in the middle of the third year he was "excluded" or perhaps withdrew voluntarily. He revolted against the rigid discipline and the barbaric treatment of the students by the teachers, whom he called "animals" in a letter to his father.

At the same time he was attracted by the Polish colony in Odesa, which was bitterly opposed to the Russian autocratic regime, and by the nascent Ukrainian movement which made him familiar with the leading authors in Ukrainian. Botev became infected with the stormy Romanticism of the day in the works of Byron, Pushkin, and Lermontov and with the revolutionary enthusiasm of Garibaldi and Bakunin. He also eagerly drank in the ideas of the Russian radical intelligentsia, Dobrolyubov, Pisarev and Chernyshevsky, and of the *narodniki* generally, as they sought to identify themselves with the peasant masses. At the end of 1865 he received from the Bulgarian community in Odesa fifty rubles and returned to Kalofer sometime in early 1867.

Here he felt himself in an alien and uncomfortable environment. His father had been taken sick and his mother was compelled to work to support the family. His parents could not look at him with favor for he had not finished the course and could not secure steady employment. Worse than that, the young man did not hesitate to condemn many teachers as harmful to the people. He denounced the efforts to create an independent Bulgarian Church as an effort to bring upon the people a new slavery and a new tyranny. On occasion and without occasion he inveighed against the life and ideals of the village as he saw them, all the while looking for a new order. He found only one sympathetic spirit, a young teacher, Parashkeva Shushulova, with whom he fell in love. Circumstances, as we learn from his poems to her, prevented marriage.

It soon became a question of removing the young firebrand from the village, lest he bring down upon the people the vengeance of the Turks for his attacks upon them and the Greek clergy. Efforts were made to have him readmitted to the gymnasium in Odesa and to have him return there in the autumn of 1867. Taking the funds given him for that purpose, he made his way instead to Sliven, Kotel, Tirnovo and Ruse and crossed the Danube to Gyurgevo to join the revolutionists in Braila in Romania.

For a while he worked in a printing house in Braila, and then he went to Bucharest to study medicine. He soon gave that up and returned to Braila to join one of the groups of armed men who were crossing the Danube to fight the Turks. The group was destroyed before he could make final arrangements to join it. He met Karavelov and also the Russian revolutionist, Sergey Nechayev, who was a pupil of Michael A. Bakunin. He accepted wholeheartedly the ideas of the Russian revolutionists and dreamed of establishing a center for smuggling illegal literature into Russia as well as Bulgaria. In a word Botev became part of the international revolutionary movement of the time. He published a journal, *The Word of the Bulgarian Émigré,* so lacking in appeal that only five numbers appeared. However, these five issues contained some of his best poems.

In the winter of 1872-3 he went to Bucharest and brought there his mother and brother (his father was already dead). He married a widow and although he was hard put to it to earn enough money to support her and his mother and brother, he did not stop for a moment his revolutionary activity. He took an active part in the journals of Karavelov, until the latter became discouraged with revolutionary work. Then he published his own organ, *Zname* (The Flag). He succeeded Karavelov as the head of the Bulgarian Revolutionary Committee but became discouraged at the failure of his enterprise and resigned without taking part in a new committee established in Gyurgevo.

In the course of 1876 Botev's name was proposed as the head of an expedition prepared to invade Bulgaria. The expedition was already organized but the original leader, Filip Totyu, had resigned because he was refused his demand for 1,000 napoleons to provide for his family if he were killed. Botev willingly consented to take his place and made his plans accordingly.

During the month of May the little company of men separated into still smaller groups and scattered to various points along the Danube. Then by prearranged agreement they boarded in different ports the river steamship, Radetski, in the guise of gardeners going to work at Kladovo. On the appointed day these separated groups which had passed unnoticed on the steamer suddenly threw off their disguise and with arms in their hands took command of the ship. They compelled the captain to steer for the Bulgarian side of the river and land them in Kozloduy on May 17, 1876. Then everything began to go wrong. The company expected reinforcements but, except for a few men from Vratsa, no one appeared. The next day the detachment moved to Borovan. Here they had the promise that they would be joined by 400 men. No one appeared. Worse than that, none of the inhabitants would give them any supplies, not even water. On the 19th, they reached the desolate and barren hill of Vola. Botev was discouraged especially when a Bulgarian shepherd demanded pay for some sheep that the men had killed and eaten. On Vola they were surrounded by a large Turkish force with two mountain guns.

The battle lasted all day and the Bulgarians repulsed the Turks with no losses to themselves. Towards evening, some of the men left their posts to secure water from a spring. Botev and his staff discussed the question of whether to continue this unequal battle without support or to try to cut their way to safety in Serbia. Just as Botev stood up to see if any new danger was threatening, a rifle bullet struck him in the heart and killed him instantly. The little force, staggered by this new misfortune, stripped his body of all identifying marks and left it behind while they sought their own safety. So ended the career of Bulgaria's great poet.

Botev was primarily a lyric poet of the Romantic and revolutionary school. The great feature of his work was his complete identification of his personal and social moods. From his early poems written in Odesa, such as *The Hayduks* and *Father and Son,* to the end of his career he identified himself with the people's cause. He made common cause with the *hayduks* in their death struggle for liberty against the *chorbadji,* who held them in financial bondage and mercilessly squeezed the last cent out of the people, and against the Turks and the Greeks, each of whom added their own exactions. To him the life of a *hayduk* engaged in constant struggle was the ideal life. He felt that the young *hayduk* who went into the mountains with his father, despite the tears and lamentations of his mother, had made the correct choice and the only one worthy of an honest and patriotic Bulgarian. Botev's own end shows his sincerity. We see it again in his ode on the execution of Vasil Levski, in which all nature mourns with Mother Bulgaria, and in *Hadji Dimitar,* when there came a rumor that the daring raider was wounded but alive somewhere in the mountains. We find it in many other poems, even in the one entitled *To My First Love,* which expresses the idea that love for a woman, no matter how passionate, cannot satisfy unless it is inextricably linked with the national cause.

A similar thought appears also in those masterpieces to his mother, *On Parting* and *To My Mother.* Into these intimate expressions of the closeness of mother and son there drifts almost imperceptibly the thought of the great mother, Mother Bulgaria, and it is hard to know where the personal emotions of the man and his views of his political and national mission merge in a greater synthesis.

He handles nature in the same way. Botev was very sensitive to natural beauty and to the charm of the Bulgarian mountains but even in his nature poems it is not only the majestic calm and peace of the mountain scenery that stirs him. The mountains are the home and refuge of the *hayduks;* their majesty reminds him of the brave and unselfish patriots who are living among them that Bulgaria may become free.

A special place in Botev's work must be devoted to his satire. With deftness and bitterness, he uses this weapon, as in *The Patriot,* to castigate those men who talk of liberty and right but who refuse to sacrifice their own lives and comfort to make those great words realities in the land. His methods are in many cases those of the Ukrainian poet Taras Shevchenko who ran the entire scale in his denunciation of the evils of Russian rule in Ukraine, although Botev had what Shevchenko did not have, a burning desire to sacrifice his life on the battlefield for his people. Equally patriotic, Shevchenko, who suffered for years as a soldier in a tsarist corrective battalion, never had the inspiration to be a soldier and to stand the actual hardships of battle for the Ukrainian cause.

Botev had the same view of religion as Shevchenko and for the same reason: bitterness against the hierarchy of an alien race. Yet Botev went further in denouncing the movement for a Bulgarian Church. He was violently anti-clerical, not so much anti-religious, as he shows in *My Prayer* in which he repudiates the old conception of a merciless God seeking out ways to punish men without administering justice to the persecutors of the common people, whose cause Botev had made his own.

Botev's poems appeared first in the various journals with which he was connected. They did not attract much attention. Even when he republished many of them in book form in 1875 along with the poems of his friend Stefan Stambolov under the title *Poems and Songs of Botev and Stambolov,* the critics paid little or no attention, though they should have seen the difference in the poetic quality of the works of the two men. The Bulgarians at home had little chance of knowing these works during Botev's lifetime. The Bulgarian émigrés in Russia and Romania were largely rich merchants and even the most ardent patriots among them were not interested in literature as such. They were busy with their own affairs and had not developed the idea of doing other things for Bulgaria than building schools in their native cities and giving some small aid to Bulgarian students in Russia and other countries. Yet no sooner had Botev attracted attention by his heroic death, than the Bulgarians awoke to the fact that he had been a great poet and a real star in the Bulgarian sky.

The Communists have greatly overstressed Botev's dependence upon Russian literature and his Russian teachers. There can be no question that he had a wide acquaintance with the Romantic poets, Pushkin and Lermontov and with the Russian *narodniki* and the radical intelligentsia of the sixties. Like the other Bulgarians who lived in the south, he was in deep sympathy with Ukrainian writers like Gogol (Hohol), Shevchenko, Kostomariv and Kvitka-Osnovyanenko. They spoke to him of another people that was, like the Bulgarians, fighting to have its culture recognized and to win its own human rights. Yet, above all, Botev drew his inspiration from Bulgarian sources and Bulgarian folklore. His past was rooted in that Bulgarian past which was both sad and glorious. He knew the Bulgarian legends and folksongs, and more than once he used the form of the traditional *hayduk* songs in his own works. As has been said of Shevchenko, he was a man who was able to compose folksongs because their spirit had so permeated his that he could play with their motifs without breaking the natural harmony and in a mysterious way he was the flowering of the traditional Bulgarian peasant culture and creativity.

Botev's prose (and he made his living as a practicing journalist) is but a commentary on his poetry and his life. He wrote only to advance the cause of Bulgaria. His works are filled with denunciations of those whom he regarded as the enemies of his people, the *chorbadji,* the Turks, the priests, the Greeks, and above all the enlighteners, all those teachers and thinkers who expected that education and education alone would bring the Bulgarians out of their oppressed state and who believed that sometime in the future the Ottoman Empire would be reformed and modernized and give a tolerable life to the Bulgarians. With these ideas in his mind, he followed events in Europe, and with sharp and often satirical pen he condemned those countries which seemed to be supporting at any given moment the Turkish position. At the same time he welcomed all those revolutionary leaders who were striving to break down the power of class and prejudice in Europe as a whole. He saw the world from the point of view of Bulgaria, for which he was ready to lay down his life.

It was this call to revolt, this glorification of the fighter for freedom that was the dominating message in Botev's short but active life. It gave added weight to all that he did. It colored every moment of his life, every word that he wrote and it showed that his final venture into his native land was not a momentary whim but the culmination of all for which he had lived and worked. How would he have fitted into a free and independent Bulgaria? No one knows, but from the day he died on that desolate Balkan hilltop, the Bulgarians discovered what they had lost. His fame is secure and his poems have been read, loved and memorized by generation after generation of Bulgarians in all walks of life and of all social classes and political orientations.

CHAPTER SIX

Ivan Vazov

If Botev flashed out like a meteor to dominate the Bulgarian literary scene for the few years before the liberation of the country, Ivan Vazov rose slowly to prominence and maintained an almost undisputed leadership as Bulgaria's foremost literary figure for the half century after the liberation. Critics in the early twentieth century might regard him as old-fashioned and limited, but he went on his way serenely, secure of his audience, the Bulgarian people. He also became the first Bulgarian author to have his works translated and thus made known abroad.

To understand the position of Vazov, we must view him against the changing background of a free Bulgaria, for in the years between the flowering of Botev and of Vazov, the Bulgarians had recovered their ancient freedom and were masters in their own house.

This independence was secured at a heavy price. The establishment of an independent Bulgarian Orthodox Church, unconnected as it was with social and political reforms, had not satisfied the Bulgarians as the Turks had expected. The demand for independence, fanned by Botev and the revolutionists, sounded louder and louder and was backed by the invasion of the country by armed detachments formed in Romania to liberate the country. In April, 1876, a widespread revolt broke out in Koprivshtitsa and found echoes north of the Balkan Mountains. The Turks, suppressing this organized movement (the April Uprising) with little trouble, then adopted a policy of terror and launched a series of massacres in areas which they supposed might become disaffected.

These massacres touched off the final spark, for they embraced the population of entire villages and offered the means for awakening the conscience of Europe, as nothing else would have done. Naturally, the Russian ambassador in Constantinople, Count Nikolay Ignatyev, exploited the situation as well as he could. At the same time Dr. George Washburn,[1] the President of Robert College in Constantinople, and Dr. Albert L. Long, the Vice-President and one of the inspirers of the Bulgarian translation of the Bible for the American Bible Society, both became aroused. They induced Eugene Schuyler, the American Consul in Constantinople and Mr. G. A. McGahan, an American journalist of Irish extraction and the representative of the *New York Herald* in Constantinople, to visit the disturbed area and to make reports.

McGahan, publishing his accounts of the massacres in the *Herald* and in the London *Daily News,* wrote:

"In England and in Europe in general people have a very wrong opinion of the Bulgarians. I have always learned, and to be frank, I myself until recently believed that they were savages no superior in point of civilization to the American Indians; you can conceive my amazement, however, when I discovered that almost every Bulgarian village had its school, and those that escaped destruction were in a flourishing shape. They are being maintained by a voluntary tax, without any (Turkish) government encouragement, but on the contrary, in spite of innumerable obstacles created by the very state authorities. Tuition in the schools is free, education is equally available both to rich and poor. It would be difficult to find a single Bulgarian child who cannot read and write. In general, the percentage of literacy in Bulgaria is not smaller than that existing in England or France."[2]

The reports of Schuyler and McGahan shocked the world and furnished the basis for the action taken by William E. Gladstone in the British House of Commons.[3] The outburst of public indignation stifled for the moment any pro-Turkish feelings and left Tsar Alexander II free to intervene on behalf of the Bulgarians.

A few months later Serbia with the tacit approval of Russia declared war on Turkey and 2,000 Bulgarian volunteers joined the Serbian army. Early in 1877 Russia, too, declared war and a Russian army, largely mobilized in the south from Ukrainians, invaded Turkey. They were joined by the Bulgarian masses who distinguished themselves in battles at Stara Zagora and at Shipka. Then, as the Russian forces advanced on Constantinople, Turkey sued for peace and, at Russia's insistence, by the Treaty of San Stefano (1878) recognized the independence of Bulgaria with boundaries satisfying most of the Bulgarian ambitions, except for the Dobrudja which Russia gave to Romania as compensation for her own occupation of Bessarabia. This triumph of Russian arms and diplomacy revived European jealousies, and a congress of great powers met in Berlin a few months later. The treaty drawn up there gave much more unfavorable terms to Bulgaria, because the powers feared that Bulgaria, thus liberated, would become merely a Russian colony. The boundaries of Bulgaria were greatly reduced and Bulgaria was recognized merely as an independent principality under Turkish sovereignty. The eastern part of the country with its capital at Plovdiv was formed into an autonomous province of Turkey under the name Eastern Rumelia. A democratic constitution was drawn up at Tirnovo for the principality which elected as its ruler Prince Alexander of Battenberg, a nephew of Tsar Alexander II (1879). However, the Russians behaved as if they were the rulers of the country. The Russian generals suspended the constitution, set up the Prince as dictator and antagonized all the Bulgarian liberals.

After the death of Alexander II, Prince Alexander restored the constitution and, in so doing, antagonized the Russians and their conservative partisans. Prince Alexander, backed by the liberals, favored the union of Bulgaria and Eastern Rumelia and, without consulting Russia, brought about this union in 1885. Russia then induced Serbia to attack Bulgaria. The Bulgarian armies won a surprising victory, and in the Treaty of Bucharest, which ended the war, the Prince received the right to appoint the governor of Eastern Rumelia and to unify its administration and army with that of Bulgaria.

Disturbed by this new development, Russia organized a conspiracy among the pro-Russian Bulgarians and Russian officers, who kidnapped the Prince, compelled him to sign an act of abdication and hustled him out of the country. Their triumph was shortlived, for a counter-revolution of the Liberals restored him to power. However, the Prince had had enough. He resigned again, this time of his own accord. Russia then submitted its own candidate, a Russian general, but the Bulgarians finally chose Ferdinand of Saxe-Coburg-Gotha (1861-1929), who was related to the dynasties of Great Britain and Belgium. In spite of all Russian intrigues, Ferdinand became Prince of a united Bulgaria in 1887. Primarily conservative in his views, he finally made peace with Russia but without burning his bridges behind him. After the Austro-Hungarian annexation of Bosnia and Hercegovina in 1908, he seized the opportunity to throw off the nominal Turkish sovereignty and restored to the Bulgarian people their long lost complete independence and established the Third Bulgarian State.

It was during this period of storm and stress and gradual stabilization of the Bulgarian political, economic and cultural life that Vazov did his work. The period called for literature of a type very different from that of the tumultuous days before the liberation; the country faced problems of a different character, and it was Vazov who gave the predominant tone to the literature of the next years.

Ivan Vazov was born in Sopot in 1850. He was less than two years younger than Botev, and yet the two men were entirely different. Botev was a born rebel and revolutionist, impatient of all restraint. Vazov was inclined to be a conservative and to reconcile himself with reality, even though that reality did not harmonize completely with his ideals. His father was a fairly well-to-do *chorbadji* and trader, not too educated or interested in education but his mother was a sensitive and artistic woman who encouraged her son's literary tastes. His father sent the young Ivan to school in Sopot and then, so that he could learn Greek and Turkish for commercial purposes, to the Plovdiv diocesan school, where the boy became acquainted with French literature and the works of Slaveykov. Much to his father's disgust, he began to write poetry, empty songs of love and nature.

In 1870 Vazov was sent to an uncle in Romania to learn business. He found occasion to visit Bucharest, Braila and Galatz. In Galatz he came into contact with the circle of Karavelov and Botev, who instilled in him an ardent Bulgarian patriotism. From this moment he became more serious and his real poetical talents began to develop. On his way back to Bulgaria in 1872, he met Slaveykov in Constantinople. Soon after, he wrote one of his better known poems, *The Pine Tree.* He taught for a while in Svilengrad, but in 1874 he was back in Sopot. Caught up in the wave of revolution, he was forced to flee after the failure of the April Uprising, and he was roused to indignation by the savage repression of the movement. Among the victims was his own father.

After the liberation, he held small political posts under Gerov and then in Ruse. He was transferred several times and finally in 1880 went to Plovdiv, the capital of Eastern Rumelia, where political and cultural life was much freer than in Sofia. He became a deputy and the president of a publishing house. He edited several newspapers and journals in which he secured the cooperation of the best writers of the time. In 1884 along with Konstantin Velichkov he published the first anthology of Bulgarian literature. All the time he was actively writing poetry and prose, developing his art, and satirizing and condemning the ignorance of many of the uneducated and almost illiterate administrators. In his writings he attacked the excessive growth of party feuds which threatened the integrity and the security of the new regime.

After the fall of Prince Alexander of Battenberg, Vazov had to flee to Russia to escape the vengeance of the new political leaders on all who had sided with the Prince and were in any way pro-Russian. There in Odesa he wrote the greater part of *Under the Yoke,* his most successful novel. He visited Moscow and St. Petersburg, returning in 1889 to Bulgaria and settling in Sofia, which had by then become the capital of the new combined Bulgaria. There he remained to the end of his life. His popularity as a writer rose higher and higher. He condemned the spread of radical ideas of a populist character, especially among the teachers, and as a conservative he called

for really constructive work. His conservatism gained him enemies but did not harm his success as a writer. For a while he served
as Minister of Education. His decisions and policies as Minister
involved him in more difficulties with the teachers and the
other leaders who wanted to introduce into the schools principles
of life and administration which he considered unsound.

When the government decided at the turn of the century to
support a policy for the liberation of Macedonia, Vazov was in
enthusiastic accord. This led him into his long series of books
and poems on the past of Bulgaria. It also insured him recognition as the Bulgarian writer *par excellence,* and for many
years he was the only Bulgarian literary man who was able
to make his entire living by his pen. His historical works in
various genres prepared the people for the Balkan Wars (which
at one time seemed to promise so much, yet ended fatally) and
for the still more disastrous entrance of Bulgaria into World
War I on the side of the Central Powers. After the defeat, he
was the only writer who ventured to express in verse the Bulgarian feelings of the moment and the sorrow that filled the
heart of every patriotic Bulgarian. He died less than a year
after the national jubilee which marked his seventieth birthday
in 1920. His death was an occasion of national mourning, and
his house in Sofia was turned into a museum.

How different this long and relatively uneventful life was
from that of Botev who died at an age when Vazov had not
yet become famous. Yet there is no Bulgarian writer who has
so fully expressed all the facets of the Bulgarian land, nature,
and people over such a long period. A romanticist by nature,
he felt a deep obligation to his people to work steadily and
consistently with his pen to make them worthy and conscious
of their own past and their contemporary position in the world.

It is very hard to classify Vazov's work or to identify him
with any school of writing, for he painted the virtues and the
vices of the Bulgarian people without resorting to panegyrics
or whitewashing their vices and at the same time without over-
stressing the negative elements as did many writers of the naturalistic school. He equally avoided the extremes of the Symbolists
of the next generation. He simply wrote of his country as he

knew and loved her, and the people, in return, read his works, even though some of the younger critics tried to deride his influence and ideas and regarded him as hopelessly outmoded. Today the Bulgarian Communists either condemn him for his failure to maintain the revolutionary fervor of his younger days and his attempts to give Bulgaria a conservative and solid government or they treat only those works which can be made to serve their purposes. So far as they can, they ignore some of his best works, the writings of his mature years, which conflict with their ideas.

In this regard they are following the example of the Russian Communist opinion of Vazov. In the *Literaturnaya Entsiklopediya,* Vol. II, pp. 73-74, we have the judgment of Moscow before World War II in the following passage:

> "Vazov served the bourgeoisie more faithfully than any other of the poets and writers of Bulgaria. During the Balkan imperialistic war, the priest of Apollo changed into a vulgar chauvinist. The grateful bourgeoisie rewarded him for it with the name of a national poet.
>
> "It was not accidental that Vazov was a member of the most reactionary party of Populists, bankers and representatives of export capital and it was not accidental that he was Minister of National Education in the cabinet of Stoilov (1897) when there fell at the hands of a murderer of this cabinet one of the most prominent Bulgarian writers—Aleko Konstantinov."

Later, when it was advisable for the Russian Communists to strengthen their hold on Bulgaria, *Pravda* in 1950 took the occasion on the one hundreth anniversary of the birth of Vazov to write (No. 7):

> "The jubilee of Vazov is a festival of democratic Bulgarian culture, which developed along the path of revolutionary national traditions under the influence of the Russian classical literature, the most advanced in the world with its high ideas. . . . Vazov revealed not only the Turkish tyranny but also those people who supported it, the bourgeois politicians of Western Europe and especially England. . . . Even

before the liberation of Bulgaria, Vazov composed a series of well-known verse full of his deep love for Russia. . . . The jubilee of Ivan Vazov contributes to the strengthening of the democratic and revolutionary traditions of Bulgarian literature and cements the friendship of the Bulgarian and Soviet peoples."

It is superfluous to state that these contradictory judgments are not due to any literary evaluation of the poet's work but are the results of the *political-literary* policy of the Kremlin.

His early collections of poems, such as *The May Garland,* still show some of the naïveté and the irresponsible nature of much of his early poetry; but with the suppression of the revolt of 1876, he wrote such poems as *The Complaints of the Mother,* which reveal the terrible conditions under which the Bulgarians were compelled to live, the *Ode to Alexander II* and the *Buried Soldiers,* which reflect the joy of the people in their final liberation.

Vazov in all of his poetical works reflects the moods of the people and their varying emotions. He does not directly and forcibly express his own feelings of the moment and his own experiences in those troubled times. Here he differs entirely from Botev in whom life and poetry were inextricably mixed. Botev's life was his poetry and his poetry was his life. Vazov, in a sense, is outside the events which he describes. Despite this detachment, he so perfectly reflects the emotions and the thoughts of his people that he gives a more vivid picture of the times than he perhaps could have done if his own personality were at the center of his work.

In the early period after the liberation he reached what may be the high point of his poetic genius when he celebrated the heroic figures of the revival in his *Epic of the Forgotten.* Here, in separate poems, he pays homage to Father Paisi, to Rakovski, the Brothers Miladinov, the actual fighters such as Levski and the volunteers who fought side by side with the Russians at Shipka. In a somewhat different vein, in the *Legends of Tsarevets,* the old palace hill in Tirnovo, he describes in ballad form all those historical events that were connected with the Second

Bulgarian Empire from its beginning to its tragic close at the hands of the Turks. Yet, even while he is glorifying the Bulgarian past, he cannot forget the tragedy of the individual that must accompany every successful victory, and in *The News* he shows how the same dispatch must carry the message of triumph and of death.

He carries this almost dualistic attitude into his poems in other fields. He shows himself thoroughly aware of the great progress that the Bulgarians made after they secured their independence, but he cannot overlook their many faults. Recognizing their patriotism and service to their people, he still saw and condemned in relatively strong language the hypocritical politicians who contrived under the cloak of idealism to serve their own interests and the interest of foreign powers. He also censured the liberated people, who all too often acted as if they were still the helpless and oppressed slaves of the days before the liberation. He condemned the quasi-intellectuals who hid their own inadequacy behind progressive slogans, as in *The Progressive*. In his philosophy he showed himself optimistic concerning the future, but at the same time in *To a Child* he painted a bleak picture of life as it is really lived. Death is a reality and it can put an end to the higher hopes of a man, but it can be disregarded for something higher. The good will ultimately prevail but only after a hard struggle, and man must not become discouraged if, for the moment, evil seems to be in the saddle. It is remarkable, too, that Vazov, who began his work with frivolous love poems, should pay so little attention to the theme of personal love in his lyric poems. Perhaps this omission was a result of his personal experience. In fact satire plays a far larger role as a weapon with which he can lash his people's defects.

He wrote a number of longer poems on romantic themes, largely unhappy, in which he pointed out the unfortunate results of arranged marriages. One of his longer, romantic works is *Zikhra,* a poem about a girl confined in a harem by the sultan lest she meet someone to love her. Here we can see clearly the romantic devices of Byron and Pushkin, although the fact that Vazov was living in a country which only a few years before knew these themes as a reality added to the poignancy of his works.

Vazov wrote many travel sketches summarizing his journeys throughout Bulgaria and to Italy. In these ecstatic sketches he gives really fresh pictures of the beauty of the Bulgarian landscape, which he felt deeply and included in many of his poems. At the same time his ability to see the humor of many situations that would have annoyed the ordinary traveller provided him with the objectivity needed to carry out his purpose of showing the Bulgarian land and people as they really were.

He uses the same methods in his many stories. Some of these, such as *The Chichovtsi,* are frankly satirical, and we cannot help laughing at the pretensions and claims of the rival village leaders as they compete for the position of overseer of the local school while their ardent admirers quarrel about Greek influence and the influence of Voltaire, subjects that they are entirely unprepared to discuss intelligently. He shows the appeal to the superstitions of the village, the elaborate system of tabus and meaningless prohibitions which have been applied to life. However, he does it all with good humor and leaves the reader with a sense not of complete despair but a consciousness that man by his own efforts can in freedom adjust these grotesque traditions and rise worthily to human dignity. He does this too in *Tsoncho's Revenge* in which a village half-wit, the butt of the entire community and especially the pretty girls, saves one of these girls from a rockfall in a cave at the cost of his own life, a sacrifice that is made voluntarily without a moment's hesitation.

He uses the same tactics in describing new Bulgaria when he scourges the self-important intellectuals for their half-baked theories. Though he was himself the son of a *chorbadji,* he could impress upon his people the dignity of honest labor on the land. In his prose as in his poetry Vazov pictured Bulgaria both as it was and as he hoped it would become.

Undoubtedly the greatest single work of Vazov was *Under the Yoke,* which he published in 1889. This describes the situation in Bulgaria in 1876 before and after the insurrection of that year. It pictures all facets of life and classes of Bulgarians of the day. It is done in the typical Vazov manner on the basis of the approved historical novel of the time, although it refers to events that took place but a few years before. Still, those years cover the period between an enslaved and an independent Bulgaria, a period which might have been decades or centuries long, so great was the difference in the state of mind that rapidly evolved even in the same individual.

The scene is the small Bulgarian city of Bela Cherkva. There appears in it a revolutionist known as Boycho Ognyanov, whose real name is Ivan Kralich. He has escaped from a Turkish prison and has chosen Bela Cherkva as the seat of his next operations because of his father's friend, the *chorbadji* Marko. After various adventures, Marko gives him false papers and makes it possible for him to stay and become the village teacher. Here, too, he wins the youth and also the love of a village teacher, Rada Gospojina, but he infuriates the leading Turkophile *chorbadji* and finally has to flee to escape arrest.

He returns on the eve of the revolution and identifies himself to his friends, Rada and Dr. Sokolov, and promises to marry Rada. Then the revolution breaks out in Klisora on April 2, 1876. Ognyanov is appointed to lead the fight and goes to Klisora. Rada also follows with a student who worships her. The peasants are aroused, but at the approach of Turkish punitive forces, they lose heart. Ognyanov escapes to Wallachia and Rada who has tried to commit suicide by blowing up the supply of gunpowder is saved and taken back to Bela Cherkva.

A little later Ognyanov, too, arrives in Bela Cherkva on the false assumption that the revolution has spread to that city. He hides in a mill and is there joined by Rada and Dr. Sokolov, but the Turks break in and kill the three.

In this novel Vazov gives a romantic picture of the tragic events of the April Uprising, showing the reaction of all classes of the population. There is the monk, the Hegumen Natanail, who is ready to use his monastery as an arsenal, and there are other priests who do not want to sacrifice themselves for the cause of the people. There are the Turkophile *chorbadji* who care only for their own safety and property. There are peasants who are willing to die for the cause but have no sense of organization or knowledge of military tactics and are easily demoralized.

Vazov even brings in the famous cannon made out of a cherry log which the peasants made and tried to use without success. Rada is a typically novelistic heroine of the nineteenth century. The reader, whether he be Bulgarian or not, can learn from the volume how the Bulgarians as a whole and individually reacted in the crisis, but Vazov very emphatically did not try to probe deeply into the psychology of even his main characters. That was not his way, for his aim was to picture events and not to explain why they occurred. Yet his method makes *Under the Yoke* good reading, and we can see why it was the first Bulgarian story to be translated into nearly all the languages of western Europe as well as Russian.

Later Vazov in a way continued the novel in another work, *The New Land.* The hero, Nayden Stremski, is the son of the *chorbadji* Marko, who was killed by the Turks. During the boy's attempt to escape he saves the life of Nevena Shamura, the daughter of an enemy of his father. He secures a post in the Russian revolutionary government in Ruse and later meets Nevena again, falls in love with her, and marries her. Stremski becomes a deputy in the Rumelian parliament and then travels in Switzerland and France. On his return to Plovdiv, the union of the two regions has taken place and on the outbreak of the Bulgarian-Serbian War, he immediately volunteers.

The novel did not win as great popularity as *Under the Yoke,* for the events which it described were the mundane ones surrounding the forming of a new and efficient government. The story lacks the appeal and the adventure of the futile revolt and the struggle for independence. The scene is basically the same but a few years later, and some of the characters who have survived reappear. It does show Vazov's personal experiences during the troublous times when the young leaders of the Bulgarian people were trying to make their new form of government function. However, it is constructed again on the principle of all of Vazov's art, and, like most continuations, it lacks the freshness of the first work.

In a third novel, *The Empress of Kazelar,* written late in the nineties, Vazov again pays his respects with considerable irony to the populist intelligentsia and contrasts with them the limited

and self-satisfied teacher Chakalov and his wife, both of whom
have no intellectual interests but desire to build up a model
economy and become rich at all costs. The novel shows Vazov's
own conservative principles. It expresses his efforts to put the
intellectual life and especially the teaching profession on a sound
basis which could offer the means for constructive work for
the people; and it makes plain that he prefers conservatism
to the stormy advocacy of doubtful doctrines.

Vazov also did for the Bulgarian theatre what he did for lyric
poetry and artistic prose. When he was in Plovdiv in the eighties,
there was a call for plays for the local theatre, and of course he
supplied the need. He dramatized some of his more romantic
stories and wrote other plays. He dramatized, too, some of his
comic sketches and produced a long series of comedies, poking
fun at the foibles of the Bulgarian people, but almost always
with that kindly attitude that was his forte. Still later he turned
to the historical drama, and in such works as *Borislav* and *Ivaylo*
he drew upon the life of the Second Bulgarian Empire to present
a picture of the Bulgarians in the past, showing in his dramas
that same facility that he exhibited in other branches of
literature.

All this assures Vazov of a unique place in Bulgarian literature.
He was a true artist, a conscientious and hard-working creator
of a new literature, which he launched on a high plane on the
world stage. No one before him had applied himself so diligently
to the field of literature. No one since has had the wide knowledge of the Bulgarian people, the wide grasp of Bulgarian life
in the past and in the present, and no one has been able to speak
with his authority and experience. There have been men of perhaps greater and deeper talent, but there has been no one
who more correctly and carefully interpreted the thoughts and
ideas of the great masses of the Bulgarian people and expressed
them in such beautiful, fluent and poetic language. It is small
wonder that Vazov on the fiftieth anniversary of his literary
career should have been greeted by all classes of the population
and the literary world, even by those critics who had previously
been his warmest opponents. We can confidently predict that

those Communist critics who today deplore his conservative tendencies and try to depreciate his influence will sooner or later also have to admit that he knew how to speak for his people and how to give them a voice commanding world attention.

CHAPTER SEVEN

The First Decades after Liberation

Ivan Vazov embodied in his works the full extent of the Bulgarian literature of the day. He was a unique phenomenon because of his range of interest and the variety of the forms of literature in which he was the master. During the half century of his activity he pictured the various phases through which Bulgaria was passing, and he alone offered a rounded picture of Bulgarian life. Yet, there were other authors who in lesser ways worked with him and presented their own views of some of the problems which the country was facing. There were still others, slightly younger, who tried to walk in Vazov's footsteps and formed, so to speak, a Vazov school, but this group appeared later and we can not fairly apply the term to Vazov's associates and contemporaries.

The problems offered by the liberation and the ensuing intrigues of the Great Powers put a heavy strain upon the small intelligentsia and subjected them to new and unexpected temptations. Before 1876 the patriots had but one ideal—to fight for a free Bulgaria. Many of these men, as we have seen, were compelled by circumstances to live abroad, to spend their lives in exile planning to set Bulgaria free, or to hazard their lives by taking part in military raids across the borders. Botev, Karavelov and Rakovski were cases in point. They were never called upon to administer a government. They engaged in true revolutionary activities, creating a tradition which lived after them even though they did not survive to see the flowering of their hopes. That tradition, which was one of violence, died hard as their successors and admirers sought to advance by the old methods their nation's cause and their own interests. The new times called for the old

94

self-sacrificing spirit but in a new type of man. However, the courses of action open to the new men lacked the glamour of the fight for freedom.

The new leaders had the unexciting and laborious task of setting up a government that would function. They had to pass and administer laws for the amelioration of conditions and convince the people to accept them. It was of little use or value, now that an independent Bulgaria had its own independent Orthodox Church, to complain endlessly of the abuses perpetrated by the Greek clergy. It was more important to make the Bulgarian Church an effective force for good. It was more important to steer the new state through the rapids of European diplomacy. The evil forces against which they had to fight arose at home: grafting politicians who looked to Turkish models of conduct, narrow-minded obscurantists and pettifoggers who tried to take advantage of the ignorance of the people who had been oppressed for centuries by foreign conquerors. They had to fight against the siren appeals of half-baked reformers, who somehow believed that they alone had the truth and tried at all costs to force these truths down the throats of the people.

In other words Bulgaria had to become a modern European state and had to accomplish this task under adverse conditions at home and pressure exerted from abroad, for both Russia and Austria-Hungary, with German backing, were trying to control Bulgarian foreign policy. Bulgaria's leaders had to struggle for real European recognition and simultaneously train their own people to be worthy of that recognition and able to use it wisely.

This situation required a new form of administrative enlightener rather than a new form of revolutionist, and that is why the Bulgarian Communists today prefer to glorify the older men whose work and lives were largely finished with the liberation and scorn those who endured the labor of the first decade following liberation. It would have been fatal to the country had the new leaders followed the old paths. This change of policy, however, colored not only the political but the literary life of the men of Vazov's generation and those born within the next ten or fifteen years.

There were so few men of higher education sufficiently trained to be administrators that responsible individuals could scarcely, as patriots, allow themselves the luxury of being only writers. Conversely there was such a small reading public in the early decades that a writer could scarcely live on the income from his works without some government post. Even Vazov was compelled to serve as Minister of Education. This precedent of the union of the administrative and literary worlds continued, with diminishing force, even down to 1939. The Bulgarian writers in the eighties and nineties, almost to a man, occupied public office for some time in their lives and had political as well as literary training. It left a definite mark upon their work.

We can take as an example a very good friend of Vazov, Konstantin Velichkov. He was born in 1855 in the city of Tatar-Pazardjik, where his father, a prominent citizen, was one of the men imprisoned by the Turks during the April Uprising. The boy did well in his studies and in 1868 was sent to the newly established Sultan's Lycée in Constantinople. Here, during six years of study, he became an admirer of French literature and especially of Victor Hugo. Here, too he began to write and translated Hugo's *Lucretia Borgia* with the aid of a friend. He became a teacher in his native city, but, caught up in the revolutionary movement, he was arrested and taken to Odrin. Later he was forced to accept various positions in Constantinople in connection with the Bulgarian Exarchate. When Bulgaria became free, he returned to Tatar-Pazardjik and held various local offices. Then he went to Plovdiv, edited a number of literary journals, met Vazov and with him prepared in 1884 the first Bulgarian *Anthology*. He became Director of National Education in Eastern Rumelia. When that province was annexed to Bulgaria and the anti-Russian disturbances began under Stefan Stambolov, he, like Vazov, was forced to flee. Unlike Vazov, however, he went to Italy, where he lived first in Florence and later in Rome. He devoted himself to studies in art and prepared a very successful series of *Letters from Rome,* one of the best descriptions of foreign countries in Bulgarian literature. His labors and the hardships of his life broke his health and compelled him to leave Italy. He went to Constantinople and then to Salonika where he taught for some years in the Bulgarian gymnasium there.

After the fall of Stambolov in 1894, he returned to Sofia and was soon appointed Minister of Communications and later of Education. He held this latter post for some years, during which he succeeded in founding an art school which became the nucleus of the Bulgarian Academy of Fine Arts, perhaps his chief monument. Later he turned his post over to Vazov because of difficulties with the teachers and became Minister of Commerce. The following year he retired from political life, and in ill health he dragged out a miserable existence until his death in 1907.

Velichkov is known in literature for his *Letters from Rome* and his translation of Dante's *Inferno*. He produced a large number of other works, both poetry and prose, much of which has been forgotten. He was not a natural poet who was able to rise to his opportunities as Vazov did. Nevertheless, his influence was not negligible in the early days, for he expressed in his own way his confidence in Bulgaria, his appreciation of the fact that Bulgarian literature should include translations of the world's masterpieces (he was a good translator) and his feeling that sacrifice for his people in the literary field was worthwhile.

The success of Vazov encouraged other men to follow in his footsteps but no one could rival him in his wide consciousness of the people as a whole and their newer and more complicated desires and needs. Perhaps the most attractive figure of this period was Aleko Konstantinov who was born in Svishtov in 1863. His father, a wealthy merchant with a keen sense of humor which his son inherited, realized the value of education. He hired private tutors for Aleko and then sent him to the school in Gabrovo. On his return, during the Russian-Turkish War, Aleko became a clerk in the office of the local governor and in 1878 went to Russia where he studied in the technical gymnasium in Mikolayiv in Ukraine. In 1881 he transferred to the University in Odesa, where, as at Mikolayiv, he paid almost more attention to literature and the theatre than to his studies.

In 1885 on his return to Bulgaria he was named a member of the circuit court in Sofia and the procurator in the Court of Appeals. His work as a judge did not take up all his time and energy. He amused himself with a group of young friends who were dubbed "Jolly Bulgaria" because of their fondness for good times, music and pranks, pursued in imitation of their gay lives in Russia. With his whimsical nature, Konstantinov could not fail to be intrigued by the humorous incongruities of the Bulgarian life of his day. Absurdities naturally abounded in a land where the peasants had not yet outgrown that frame of mind which had been developed by centuries of Turkish oppression and yet were trying to adapt their lives to the pattern which their leaders had introduced from western Europe. Konstantinov put these absurdities into literary form. He took his political work seriously and was scandalized in his humorous way when a government partisan called on him for a stern condemnation of the editor of an anti-government newspaper. He soon was relieved of his post and busied himself as a lawyer, but he had small taste for this profession.

He spent on his translations from Pushkin, Lermontov, Molière, and other foreign authors almost more time than he did on his legal practice. The money that he received from his writing he set apart for travelling. Thus in 1889 he visited Paris, in 1893 Prague and the United States, and somewhat later he conceived the idea of a trip around the world. On all of his travels he maintained the same attitude of mind, a whimsical form of Rousseauism and a capacity for detecting the folly of the social order.

On his return from Chicago he was drawn into politics. He planned to unite the various democratic parties into a strong opposition against the conservatives, who supported at all costs the arbitrary power sought by Prince Ferdinand. His activities aroused the hostility of the military class, as did those of his friend Mikhail Takev, who stirred up still more hatred by his political actions. One evening when the two friends were in a restaurant, three murderers attacked Takev. They failed in their attempt on Takev but mortally wounded Aleko Konstantinov who died May 11, 1897 when he was only thirty-four years of age.

Konstantinov's first important prose work was *To Chicago and Back,* an account of his reflections on his journey to America. He eagerly devoured all that there was to see in the, for him, exotic civilization of the United States and the peculiarities of the Chicago World's Fair. He combines his whimsical observations with a great deal of shrewd common sense, and this makes his work valuable as a foreigner's view of the American foibles and weaknesses of that time.

Even more successful was his collection of stories dealing with Bay-Ganyu. This is perhaps the most popular satirical collection in Bulgarian literature. Aleko Konstantinov somewhat changed his conception of the character when he republished the series of journalistic sketches in book form. However, basically Bay-Ganyu remains the same: a man of incredibly bad taste in all aspects of life, an incorrigibly ignorant man unable to appreciate any of the finer things of life or to estimate correctly a situation in which he finds himself, but at the same time a man with an uncannily developed cunning who is able to extricate himself from all the unpleasantnesses which he encounters because of his unmitigated gall and his refusal to face facts as they really are. And what a mass of difficulties he plunges into! Bay-Ganyu visits the palace, he runs elections, he is ready to tackle any problem no matter how involved, for he is sure that he alone has the key to its solution. Cringing and haughty, he moves through life in his own way, and the reader can hardly resist the feeling that there never could be such a character as Bay-Ganyu, at the same time realizing that he has personally known in his own experience far too many of such mortals. Later Bay-Ganyu goes to Europe. There again he does everything wrong and yet lands regularly on his feet.

The stories are satirical in a true sense, but Konstantinov treats his hero with a mellowness and understanding which save Bay-Ganyu from being pilloried as a man entirely beyond the pale. The author never forgets, in his sternest condemnations, to emphasize some human touch that softens his merciless criticism. Bay-Ganyu is in fact, like many of his contemporaries, groping to find his way with old, familiar methods through the complexities of a newly developing, unfamiliar state order imported from more developed countries abroad. It is small wonder that this picture of the unparalleled, semi-intelligent, and grotesque figure should remain a favorite among all classes of Bulgarians, even though they no longer see Bay-Ganyus in their crudest form walking the streets of Sofia and playing their part in high governmental offices.[1]

Aleko Konstantinov showed the same whimsical touch in his *feuilletons,* which he wrote to further his political program, but he was fundamentally too kindly to condemn without some human touch or explanation any of the vices of his fellow-countrymen, whether in the social or political sphere. His early death was one of the great losses of Bulgarian literature in the nineteenth century.

In his genial attitude toward his fellow-man Konstantinov differs sharply from his older compatriot, Stoyan Mikhaylovski, who was born in Elena in 1856 in a well-educated family. He studied at Elena and Tirnovo and then attended the French lycée in Constantinople where he completed the course in 1872. Here he acquired an excellent knowledge of French and of French culture, and after a couple of years in Doyran in Macedonia he went to France and studied from 1874 to 1879 in the Université Bouches de Rhône. During the struggle for liberation he returned for a while to Bulgaria but soon went back to France to finish his studies.

Then he became a lawyer in Tirnovo and was later appointed a judge first in Svishtov and then in Sofia, where he filled various distinguished posts. He soon retired on a pension, more or less disgusted with the course of government and of affairs in general, living an embittered life in solitude until his death in 1927.

Mikhaylovski had an excellent knowledge of French life and literature, but it is hard to know whether he ever had any understanding of either. His French coloring was developed rather as a cover for his ardent Bulgarian patriotism and his desire to use French forms to castigate the evils of Bulgarian life and politics. In an enormous mass of books, poems, and pamphlets he poured out without mercy his aversion to things as they were with never a thought of making his ideas palatable for his readers. He was not a deep or a consistent thinker, but when the spirit came upon him, he lashed out at whatever aroused his ire, without caring whether his satirical attacks were too extreme to achieve the end which he sought. Thus with equal fervor he struck out in thunderous blows at the politicians, the press, literature, and the writers. Nothing escaped his withering scorn and sarcasm.

This constant preoccupation with the evils of the moment dated his works and prevented later generations from according his technical and linguistic skill the appreciation they deserved. Mikhaylovski lacked conspicuously that spirit of urbanity and humor that made the works of Vazov and Konstantinov amuse the people even while they scourged and ridiculed the vices of the day. As a result, Mikhaylovski's work, although he was unquestionably one of the great writers of the period immediately after the liberation, did not remain alive and vital as did the other writing of the period.

A more engaging figure is that of Todor Genchov Vlaykov, who wrote under the pen-name of Venelin, borrowed from the distinguished, early friend of Bulgaria. He was born in Pirdop in 1865. From his early years he fostered a certain inherited religious sense and interest which was to last all his life. He passed through the schools of Pirdop, but, having to pursue his studies elsewhere during the struggle for liberation, he went to Sofia. He had already become interested in poetry, partly through a not too skilled teacher and partly through a volume of Vazov's early poems which he secured from an itinerant book salesman. Some of his own experiments in imitation of Vazov he published in 1883 under the title *Macedonian Tears*. It was in Sofia that he met some future writers and critics and began to compose short stories.

On finishing at the gymnasium Vlaykov had the opportunity to travel on a fellowship to the West, but he preferred to go to Moscow where he entered upon the study of philology. He had to return to Bulgaria during the Bulgarian-Serbian War of 1885, but he soon went back to Russia. He developed greater interest in the literary, political, and religious writings of the day than he did in pure philology. His works show definitely the influence of Pisarev and Chernyshevsky, the religious and moral teachings of Tolstoy, and above all, the writings of the older generation of Ukrainians: Shevchenko, Gogol (Hohol), and Kvitka-Osnovyanenko who presented sympathetically and often whimsically the life of the peasants of Ukraine. It was under their influence that he wrote his first story, *The Granddaughter of Grandfather Slavchov,* which he sent back from Russia for publication in Bulgaria.

His sympathies with the people and his convictions, strengthened by the ideas of the Russian *narodniki,* made him feel that he had to serve the people, but, unable to make a living by his pen alone, he became a teacher in Pirdop. Later he conceived the idea of burying himself in a village and sharing, as a teacher, the lives of the ordinary people. However, his friends dissuaded him, and he became for a while a school inspector in Sofia. Then, a change of politics removing him from that position, he became a teacher of Russian and Bulgarian in the III Men's Gymnasium in Sofia. He continued to write but was soon drawn into politics and joined the democratic group around Aleko Konstantinov. He failed to be elected to the Sobraniye, but he became the political editor of the organ of a new Radical Party and for almost twenty years he gave up literature. On his retirement from journalistic work after thirty years of service, he resumed writing .In his last years he became blind but still continued to take a deep interest in religious and ethical questions and was the unquestioned dean of Bulgarian writers. He died in 1943.

Vlaykov's stories, though they bear the unmistakable imprint of the Ukrainian tales of Kvitka-Osnovyanenko, are thoroughly Bulgarian and stress the life of the people in its changing aspects. The stories, partly idealistic and partly realistic, one and all stress the positive qualities that Vlaykov admired in the peasant —his love of labor, his stubborn pursuit of a definite goal, his love for his family and his high regard for chastity in love. Vlaykov's writings reflect the agricultural and official life of his own village. Using relatively simple forms, he shows the tragedies that confront and overwhelm man because of his own failures and, in some cases, because of social forces which are not under his control but are the result of the defects of society.

The vast majority of his stories contain positive characters with qualities and virtues which shine through the defeats that they have to meet, as in *The Life of a Mother,* in which the central character is overwhelmed by the events of life. He pictures the disintegration of the old patriarchal existence, as in *Uncle Stoyko,* or some slow destruction of a formerly cherished ideal, but he writes without denying the values of the past or condemning too strongly the shifting course of events.

Whatever the mood of Vlaykov's stories, the gentleness of his character and his firm grip upon religious and ethical ideals can never be overlooked. His writing shows a later stage of peasant development than many of Vazov's works but, like his teacher, he never loses sight of the fact that it is his task to help the people by presenting to them the ideal side of Bulgaria as a call to increased activity in fruitful and progressive ways.

The last of this group of writers, Anton Strashimirov, while perhaps second only to Vazov in his knowledge of Bulgaria and its problems, was such a stormy and irascible soul that he was perpetually in conflict with someone or other. He never received the full recognition that would have been his, had he more closely defined his purposes in writing. He was born in 1872 in Varna where his father had fled to escape Turkish persecution. His father died when the boy was seven, and the young Anton was brought up by a bachelor uncle. When he had finished the second class in school, he started to wander and from that time supported himself by all kinds of jobs, from painting and serving in an inn to working in a tobacco factory and a printing firm. In 1888 he went back to Varna and finished another grade of school while living with a married sister. The wanderlust again came over him, and he landed in a school in Shumen where his brother was a teacher. He succeeded in passing the fourth class, thanks to his brother, and entered the fifth. Then his brother planned to send him to the Sadovsko Agricultural School abroad, but he would not stand the life and left after two months. He started to teach but failed, being dropped from all the school positions which he secured for rudeness, incivility or brawling. In 1892, on the advice of his brother, he gave up his attempts at writing poetry and wrote his first story, *Dulchev,* which was published in a newspaper in Tatar-

Pazardjik. In 1895, after more unpleasantnesses stemming from his political activity, he went to Berne, Switzerland for two years, where he studied literature and geography. On his return he again secured a teaching position in Kazanluk, but within a year he was barred from all teaching in Bulgaria because of his unruly character.

Strashimirov then settled in Sofia and dabbled in politics. He worked on a long succession of newspapers, in which he published not only his political articles but a large number of his literary works. He threw himself into the Macedonian cause. In 1911 he became a member of the National Assembly, but again his unruly and undisciplined character kept him from rising in the government ranks, whatever party was in power.

He had lived in all parts of Bulgaria. He had worked in some capacity in the villages and in the cities, and had acquired an excellent understanding of the evils of the day, the defects of the governmental and social system. He could have devoted himself to consistent work either in *belles-lettres* or in the political field, but he chose neither. The result was that at times his writings showed flashes of brilliancy, and at times he allowed his social indignation to interfere with the unity and harmony of his literary work. This was his tragedy. Yet, his prose and dramas were often honored by the Academy of Sciences and produced in the National Theatre. In 1922, under the peasant regime of Stamboliyski, the Ministry of Education published an anthology of his works, and he planned other reprints of his sketches. Still he did nothing consistently. He died in 1937.

In the preface to his first volume, *Laughter and Tears* (1897), he said:

"These stories written throughout six years in the wretched homes of the people, did not arise to the melody of the 'honeyed' shepherd's pipe—that has long been driven from the daily life of the people, driven out by the hard evils of centuries. In them are mixed the laughter and the tears of a young man, permeated with an idea and illusions like those of the mass of the people who are now crushed by the new conditions but are still unchangeable as they have been throughout the centuries."

Strashimirov told the truth. In his pictures of the life of the Bulgarian village, he was prone to stress the dark sides rather than to mingle his gloomy accounts with tales of the peasants' lighter moments.

And what a picture he was able to present, for he knew the life that he described with all of its hardships. In fact in some of his early works he was so intent upon describing these difficulties that he seemed to lose all sense of literary values. Yet he could be more optimistic. In the story entitled *Autumn Days* we have a young man, Doyno Maydovski, courting a girl named Angelina. She loves Djonka whose family is hostile to hers. After various episodes Djonka is forced to flee to the mountains. Maydovski, the approved suitor, prepares the marriage, but Angelina jumps out of the window. She too disappears in the mountains. Here she fortunately meets her lover and the story ends happily with the two united and the family feud at an end.

Strashimirov does not, however, confine himself to the village. He plunges into the problem of the cities and their submerged classes. He shows some appreciation of their social and psychological problems and the value of the new ideas which were slowly spreading in all classes of society.

His dramas show the same features. One of the most effective of these, *The Vampire,* shows a clash between an old tyrannical woman and a young man. She has picked him as her daughter's husband, without any regard for the girl's feelings. The marriage takes place but when Vela refuses to give up her true lover, the jealous husband flees to the mountains and joins a band of outlaws. He is by now convinced that the old woman is responsible for his plight. When he and the outlaws come down to the village, he kills the lover, but the old woman is physically strong enough to escape and hands him over to the authorities. *The Vampire* is one of the striking plays in the Bulgarian repertoire. It shows very well that when Strashimirov allowed himself to develop his theme logically and consistently, he could do it with real art and that he possessed a talent which many of his enemies refused to recognize.

There were minor figures in the period, such as Mikhalaki Georgiev, who are now almost forgotten. All of these authors showed themselves aware of the needs of the Bulgarian people and attempted both by their public activity and their literary work to meet these needs. They often fell between the two stools and did not succeed in either endeavor. Yet, their work shows a definite advance over the pre-liberation writers. Without belonging to any particular school, they prepared the people for the new literary movement that was to follow.

CHAPTER EIGHT

The Coming of Modernism

As we have seen, the writers of the first two decades of Bulgarian independence were compelled to make their living in diverse occupations and to work in the two fields of politics and literature. Because the number of trained men in the newly liberated country was too small to answer the vital needs of administration and culture, authors, even against their will, were forced to play an active role in political life. By the nineties, the situation had begun to change. The younger group of literary men were able to devote themselves entirely to literature, deflected from their course only somewhat by service of some kind in the Bulgarian National Library in Sofia and the other cultural institutions.

Yet we cannot draw a hard and fast line between the older and the younger men; some of the latter differed more by training than by age from their elders. They had had the opportunity to pursue literary studies abroad, largely in western Europe, and, except for those who had imbibed the doctrine of Marxism, they tended to discount the Russian political and theoretical adherents of revolution. The two men who led this younger group and prepared the literary defence of the new attitude were Pencho Slaveykov and Dr. Krest Kristev, the one an outstanding poet and the other a literary critic. Both men were under the influence of advanced German modernism and in the Communist jargon of the present day have been dubbed "bourgeois individualists."

Pencho Slaveykov was the fifth son of the old writer and poet, Petko Rachev Slaveykov. He inherited his father's poetic gifts, although he used them very differently. Born in Trevna in 1866, he was only three years younger than Aleko Konstantinov and six years older than Strashimirov. In his early years he was largely brought up by his mother, for his father was engaged in literary and political work in Constantinople. However, he could remember his father's role at the time, his service as a guide to General Skobelev and the burning of his father's house and manuscripts in Stara Zagora in 1876-7. The boy received his early education in various places in Bulgaria, especially Plovdiv, which in the early eighties was the center of Bulgarian cultural life. He was taken to Sofia in 1885. Before this he had suffered various severe illnesses, both pneumonia and typhus, and the ensuing complications made him for years an almost hopeless invalid. He was sent to Vienna and Paris for treatment, but he never fully recovered his health. It was his father's help and sympathy that encouraged him to persevere in study despite his physical handicaps.

During these years he acquired a good knowledge of Russian literature, and he also became familiar with the works of Heine through a Russian translation. In 1892 he went to Leipzig to study literature and philosophy and remained in that city until 1908. Though he travelled extensively in the various Slavic regions, it was German influence that remained paramount in his works and it was through German that he became familiar with all of the cultural advances in western Europe. His chief models were Goethe, Heine, Schopenhauer and Nietzsche. Although these men influenced his ideas, he never became a slavish adherent of any of them. He was not attracted to the extreme ideas of the French decadents, but he did learn to appreciate the careful workmanship of the younger European authors and joined in their revolt against the positivism and naturalism which were the prevailing trends. He was also attracted to Nietzsche's theory of the superman but not in its crudest form.

In 1908 Pencho Slaveykov returned to Bulgaria to live and during the next years held various posts in the Bulgarian National Library and the National Theatre. Yet, he was too independent for the political authorities and was relieved of several posts. In a sense this depressed him and isolated him from the life of the country. Finally he took a trip to Italy where, on the Lago di Como, he had a stroke in 1912 and passed away at the age of forty-six. In 1921 his body was returned to Bulgaria, where he had already been recognized as a great poet.

With his friend, Dr. Kristev, Pencho Slaveykov took an advanced position in the struggle to broaden Bulgarian cultural life and to implant in the native tradition the general principles of European art and culture. This led to a bitter literary controversy between the supporters of Vazov and the older writers with their realism and populist ideals and the newer psychological and philosophical school of Pencho Slaveykov and Dr. Kristev and their chief literary organ, *Misl* (Thought). Both sides took extreme positions regarding the future and purpose of literature. Later, more sober thought included the realization that there were elements of right and truth in both camps. However, the present regime in Bulgaria has gone as far as it can in criticizing Slaveykov and his group for their neglect of the Russian revolutionary writers of the nineteenth century and their insistance upon the rights of the individual. As a matter of fact, the entire development of Bulgarian literature in the pre-liberation and post-liberation days was a vehement assertion of the principle that the Bulgarians, after centuries of oppression, had much to learn from abroad. Nevertheless, in the fervor of liberation and despite the political turmoil of the nineties, the writers were all too often satisfied with what they had accomplished. They needed some new inspiration from outside to move to still more advanced positions. This inspiration was furnished by Pencho Slaveykov, and, after reflection, the younger men did not deny the accomplishments and successes of the older writers.

What Pencho Slaveykov wanted and succeeded in doing in his own work was to breathe into Bulgarian poetry a philosophical as well as a lyrical and descriptive element for this had been lacking in the more artless works of his predecessors, including those of his own father. This philosophical content did not form a consistent whole. Pencho, even in his first immature collection of poems, *A Young Man's Tears* (1888), stressed the idea that the heart is governed by different motives and laws than the reason, and this inconsistency runs through all of his further work.

In Leipzig he developed his innate pessimism still further,

adopting Heine's theory of the hedonism of suffering. He was perhaps influenced by his own years of ill health, but he could find external support for the theory through the experiences of such men as Beethoven, who became deaf and never heard any of his finest works of music. Yet, this principle, as he expressed it in his poems of *Prometheus,* who suffered because of his services to mankind, could not satisfy him. He turned to the story of *Phryne,* whose perfect beauty won her the pardon that she could not have otherwise hoped to receive. Thus Slaveykov wavers in an irrational hesitation between his belief in the power of suffering and in the beauty of art.

His search for a solution to this philosophical dilemma is reflected in his *Epic Songs* of the first series (1897) and the second (1907). The two collections reveal Slaveykov's philosophical development during his stay in Leipzig. They reflect also his appreciation of the basic feelings and traditions of the Bulgarian people, who bowed to a sober realism which their sense of idealism urged them not to accept. With his lack of philosophical consistency, Slaveykov tried to create a synthesis of the real and the ideal, avoiding the use of metaphysical devices to bring this about and rather relying upon some incomplete fusion through the different laws and modes of operation of the heart and the reason.

In 1907 he published a lyric collection, *The Dream of Happiness.* As he expresses it in one poem of this collection, "my soul is strange to the world like an ancient temple in ruins, but the world in its confusion seeks to enter it, only in order to profane it." Here his mood is that of the Romantic Russian poet, Lermontov. Yet, Slaveykov does not seek an absolute isolation. In the day he wishes for the night and in the night for the day. He wishes to combine the real and the dream. This collection shows the marked influence of Heine, but even while he is most dependent upon Heine's spirit, Slaveykov remains firmly himself in his search for a new philosophical content which will aid him in making clear to his people the beauty of the world and of human nature despite his pessimism about both.

In his next collection, *On the Islands of the Blessed* (1910), he passed into a new phase in which, to some degree, he corrected but did not deny his former thinking. This work is an anthology of poems by various writers which Slaveykov corrected and amplified by speaking in his own person, although, to secure his effects, he often introduced poems of his own as the writings of unknown poets. These poems reflect his pantheism, a pantheism with a definitely Christian coloring, even though he seems not to accept some of the basic ideas of Christianity. He tries in his own way to unite the Superman and the God-man, the one looking out from the world and the other looking into it. This attempt on philosophical grounds to unite God and man is one of the keys to that philosophical thinking which, in various forms, runs through all of his work.

The last and greatest of the works of Pencho Slaveykov was his *Song of Blood,* which he had not finished at the time of his death, although he had worked on it for all of his poetical life. It was inspired probably by the memories of his father and also by such novels as Vazov's *Under the Yoke.* In it Slaveykov attempted to present the philosophical and psychological basis of the Bulgarian movement for independence. The poem is a description of the April Uprising with its culmination in the battle of Shipka, but the poet was more interested in the delineation of the motives of his individual characters and of the people as a whole than he was in the description of the actual course of events. He tried to do for Bulgaria what Mickiewicz had done for Poland in *Pan Tadeusz*—to create a national epic for his people and to describe that people as the chosen of God not only in their hours of success but in their centuries of oppression. It was the national endurance of that oppression that made the nation a Prometheus with a hope for the future; the poet wanted to glorify its possibilities rather than create a Bulgarian Messianism, either on the Russian or the Polish pattern. He wove into his work strands of his individual thinking and his favorite themes, the results of his reading of Tolstoy and Nietzsche. He also employed motifs of the folksongs and folk traditions which he had learned in his early youth under the influence of his father, who had taken an important part in the Bulgarian fight for independence. How he would have finished and revised the book we cannot say, but fragmentary as it is, this work remains perhaps his greatest and most ambitious monument and the one which brought him the closest to the Bulgarian national spirit and the ordinary Bulgarian citizen.

In addition to his poetical works, Pencho Slaveykov, in a large number of articles in *Thought,* outlined the theoretical bases of his belief in art and in the duties and responsibilities of the artist. It was his conviction that the artist, in his actions and work, is bound to fulfill not the standards of the mob but the eternal standards of right, beauty and truth expressed through his artistic conscience. This was a direct challenge to the views of the older generation, which had fixed its gaze upon the well-being of the nation and the preparation of the nation to play a significant role in European politics.

We can thus see Pencho Slaveykov's role in Bulgarian literature. He was the first of a large number of authors who learned abroad the secrets of the European poetical culture of the last half of the nineteenth century and tried to acclimate it in the Bulgarian soil. His methods and his goal could not win him the popularity which was won so easily by his father and Vazov. Yet he played an important part in the development of the Bulgarian literary consciousness and spread the seeds of that movement which was to gain world recognition for Bulgarian literature. It is small wonder that his friends felt justified in presenting his name for the Nobel Prize in Literature on the eve of his untimely death, when he was still in possession of his poetical powers.

Pencho Slaveykov was the creative artist who breathed life into the new ideas and exemplified them in practice. The theoretician was his friend, Dr. Krest Kristev, born of a Bulgarian family in Pirot in 1866 and given the Serb name of Stavro Kristich. When Pirot was handed over to the Serbs by the Treaty of Berlin, his family moved to Sofia, and he took the equivalent Bulgarian name of Krest Kristev. In 1885 he went to Leipzig to study literature and philosophy and received the doctorate there in 1888. On his return to Bulgaria, he taught for two years in Kazanluk and then was appointed to the Highest School in Sofia, the institution that was soon to become the University of Sofia. Here he was Instructor in German and Professor of Philosophy until he was removed for political reasons. He was later reappointed a couple of times. In Sofia he busied himself with editing various journals, first *Kritika* (Criticism), but his great work was as editor of the journal, *Misl* (Thought), which for seventeen years was the organ of the advanced forms of literature and the chief medium for the younger writers. On the eve of World War I, Dr. Kristev protested against the policy of the Bulgarian government and was arrested. After his release he continued his work, but the disastrous defeat of Bulgaria broke him down and he died in 1919.

He was the first serious literary critic in Bulgarian literature. He had studied in Germany not only German philosophy but also the theory of literature. On his return home, he endeavored to apply the principles which he had learned to the literature of his native land. In the earlier part of his career he described the problems of esthetics, and his criticism of books was explanatory and descriptive. Later he began to criticize the general theories on which the authors were working, and he led a particularly vigorous campaign against the later works of Vazov, whom he charged with neglect in his later years of those finer sides of art which he had known so well how to stress in his earlier and greater works.

Kristev, developing a theory of a spiritual aristocracy among writers, declined to give full credit to many of the older men who did not in his opinion come up to the standards which he had set. His favorite authors and those whom he praised most highly were the group of Modernist poets headed by Pencho Slaveykov. He saw in them the recognition and fulfillment of the cultural possibilities of the Bulgarian people, something that was lacking in too many of the older writers. Naturally the present Bulgarian regime looks with disfavor at Dr. Kristev. He is accused of fostering individualism and fascism, ideas which in their present interpretation were alien to him because he always laid his emphasis on the production of artistic works which could not be turned out on an assembly line of literature.

We must mention here another scholar who had much to do with the development of Bulgarian literature and culture and laid a firm basis in philology and ethnology for the work of the younger writers. This man was Professor Ivan Shishmanov. He was born in Vidin in 1862 but as a boy, after his father's death, he had the opportunity to study in Vienna, where he remained from 1876 to 1882. On his return to Bulgaria he taught for a while at Vidin and then secured a post in the Ministry of Education. Here he had the possibility of studying on a fellowship at Jena. To improve his French, he next went to Geneva, Switzerland, where he stayed, with some interruptions, for a year.

While he was there, he became friendly with the family of Mykhaylo Drahomaniv and later married Drahomaniv's daughter. He returned to Sofia and had a long and brilliant career as a professor at the University of Sofia in various fields of ethnology and literature. During 1918-1919 he served as Bulgarian envoy in Kiev to the Ukrainian National Republic. After the conquest of that state by the Communists, he returned to Sofia and resumed his work. He died suddenly while attending a scientific meeting in Sweden in 1928. His studies were important, but perhaps his greatest accomplishment was his success in securing for his father-in-law a position as Professor in the then new University of Sofia. Mykhaylo Drahomaniv, or Dragomanov, (1841-1895) was one of the outstanding Ukrainian scholars and patriots of the second half of the nineteenth century. He had been Professor of History in the University of Kiev and had published several works on Ukrainian ethnology, folklore and folksongs. In 1876 he was deprived of his professorship in an anti-Ukrainian movement on the part of the Russian government. At the same time a *ukaz* of Tsar Alexander II prohibited the printing of books in Ukrainian. Drahomaniv went to Switzerland as an emissary of the Ukrainian circles and printed in Geneva the journal *Hromada* (Community). For the next ten years he was the spokesman for the Ukrainian cause in western Europe and brought it to the attention of the western world. It was during this time that Shishmanov met him. Drahomaniv, an outstanding scholar, a progressive but moderate thinker, was sharply critical of many of the Russian revolutionary ideas[1] and worked for the cooperation of the various Slavic peoples. He taught Shishmanov and his other students in Bulgaria his spirit and methods, and he did much to establish Bulgarian scholarship on a firm basis.

It was still more important to Bulgaria that his niece, Larysa Kosach,[2] better known by her pen name Lesya Ukrainka, spent considerable time in Sofia with her uncle and cousins. She was an exponent of precisely those new moods and methods that Dr. Khristev and Pencho Slaveykov were calling for, and now in Sofia she had the opportunity to impress her ideas independently upon many of the younger Bulgarian writers. Thus, although Ivan Shishmanov always remained more of a scholar than a literary man, it was through his direct and indirect connections that many innovations were made in Bulgarian literature, and the national culture was deepened and advanced.

The second of the outstanding poets of this modernist group was Peyo Yavorov, a man of great emotional variations but a consistent lyric poet and perhaps even greater and more purely lyrical than Pencho Slaveykov. His father, Totyu Kracholov, apparently of Arab descent, had for various reasons settled in the city of Chirpan and here Peyo was born in 1878. He was a secluded, retiring, and delicate child throughout his school career. Later he went to a gymnasium in Plovdiv, but his father suffered financial reverses and had to take him out of the school before he finished the course. The boy then became in 1898 a student telegrapher in his native city, and the next year he was sufficiently trained to become a regular telegrapher.

Before he started to study telegraphy he paid a visit to Sofia in the autumn of 1895 in the hope of securing a position in the literary or theatrical world. He failed in both endeavors. Although he did secure a certain entrée into the literary field, he became far more absorbed in socialism, and for the next years he preached this doctrine very energetically. He became the editor of *Delo* (The Cause) when his friends called him to Sofia in 1901 as the chief of one of the telegraph and post offices. Then he gave this up to join a revolutionary detachment in Macedonia, which was struggling at the moment to join Bulgaria and win independence from Turkey. He fought there for almost two years with his friend Gotse Delchev. On his return to Bulgaria he took the editorship of another journal, *Mace-*

donia, and then became head librarian in the Bulgarian National Library in Sofia. In 1906 Shishmanov, who was then Minister of Education, sent him to Paris, after he had made a trip on his own to Vienna and Geneva. In 1908 he became associated with the Bulgarian National Theatre and wrote for it his two plays, *In the Foothills of Vitosha* and *When the Thunder Strikes.*

His works almost without his own effort received the approval of Slaveykov and Dr. Kristev, who published many of the writer's best poems in *Thought.* In fact it was they who induced him to take the pen name of Yavorov. Unfortunately, this man of great promise was not destined to a long life.

He fell in love in 1907, but circumstances prevented marriage. Then a little later he met another girl, the daughter of a wealthy provincial family. This love affair tortured him, for the family did not approve of his socialistic ideas. There is no way of knowing how it would have developed. The girl joined him in Paris on his visit there and died suddenly. This threw the poet into the depths of despair. At the same time a third girl, Lora Karavelova, set her heart upon marrying him and also followed him to Paris and proposed while he was still overwhelmed with grief. She did not accept his refusal and continued to follow him. He finally yielded in 1912 on the eve of the First Balkan War. The poet returned safely from his military service, but married life proved difficult for both partners and Lora finally committed suicide. Dazed and crushed by this, Yavorov tried to shoot himself but succeeded only in injuring one eye. This injury resulted in total blindness. During this period some of his ill-wishers circulated the story that he had murdered his wife. This was more than he could stand and on October 17, 1914 he shot himself again. This time his attempt at suicide was successful. Thus died at the age of thirty-six one of Bulgaria's greatest poets.

Yavorov began to write poetry under very unfavorable conditions. During his years as a telegrapher and after his first discouraging visit to Sofia, he commenced to read diligently all of the great Russian classics and the Russian radical literature as well as Heine in a Russian translation. His poems, published in the socialist *Delo,* reflected very keenly the poet's dissatisfaction with his own lot and also his social indignation at the downtrodden conditions of the Bulgarian peasants, for whom he had more sympathy than he had for the proletariat of the growing Bulgarian cities. In a sense he swung between the influence of Lermontov, with his demonic feeling concerning his own ability and suffering and lack of immediate recognition, and the influence of Nadson, the favorite of the Russian radicals of the eighties and nineties with his outflowing of love for the oppressed and his feeling that however bad the present was, the future would somehow have to be better, even though he had no idea how the improvement would come to pass. These early poems with the usual socialistic themes nevertheless revealed Yavorov's growing mastery of metre and a growing note of personal lyricism that attracted the attention of such men as Pencho Slaveykov and Dr. Kristev. It was not too long before he was asked to contribute to their journal *Thought*. It is these early poems that have endeared Yavorov to the Bulgarian Communists. At the same time, these very poems called forth severe criticism from Slaveykov, who in a preface to an edition of the poems issued in 1904 pointed out the surprising lapses from good taste in his social themes. Yet even Slaveykov admired the poet's expression of his personal feelings and of his keen appreciation of the beauties of nature. All this assured Yavorov of a special place in Bulgarian literature and encouraged him to develop his real talent, his amazing control of the metrics and the sounds of the language and his skill in pure lyric poetry. Such poems of this period as the *Crocus, Spring* and *May* have a dominant lyric and wistful note, jarred now and then when Yavorov expresses his own views on the hard lot of the peasant.

His trip to Macedonia marked the beginning of a new period. He became a great admirer of Gotse Delchev, one of the leaders of the Macedonian movement. After Delchev's death Yavorov published his biography in thoroughly lyric prose. Later he wrote the *Hayduk Couplets,* a prose account of his wanderings as a *chetnik*[3] and his own experiences and emotions. His experiences as well as his *Hayduk Songs* brought the work of Yavorov into close connection with that of Botev and the early fighters for Bulgarian liberty, but they also gave him a new place in

Bulgarian literature and freed him from the burden of his formerly narrow socialistic views and aspirations.

By 1907 when he published his collections, *Insomnia* and *Visions,* after his return from Nancy, Yavorov began to find himself, and, without adopting the deep philosophical thought of Slaveykov, he handled in his own way the cursed questions of life and death in a lyrical form. This maturity is true of his last collection, *The Breath of the Shadows on the Clouds* (1911), in which he stresses the ephemeral character of all things existing. In these later works his poems show some influence of the contemporary school of Russian Symbolists, reflecting such writers as Balmont and Merezhkovsky. In some poems based upon historical or quasi-historical personages, such as Messalina, Cleopatra and Sappho, he points out how their deep emotions were concentrated on some shadowy, if not altogether imaginary, figure and yet did not lose their deep truth and reality. These later works showed the genius of Yavorov at its best, and in the harmony and beauty of his thought and style he reveals little or nothing of the terrible discord and the waves of despair that were destroying his vitals and making his life intolerable.

In 1910 he brought out his first drama which was produced successfully in the National Theatre, *In the Foothills of Vitosha.* The drama in a sense reflects one of his own unhappy love affairs, for he presents the young idealistic radical Kristoforov running for political office and being defeated by the representative of the propertied classes, Stepan Dragodanoglu. Unfortunately Kristoforov loves Mila, a younger sister of Stepan. The proposed marriage is frowned upon by the family who place her under restraint and try to find for her a more suitable husband, of a conservative type. Kristoforov cannot agree to yield his independence to the political demands of the Radical Party to which he belongs and retires from politics. At the same time Mila, who has not had the courage to break with her family and marry him, escapes from them but is run down by a street car on her way to find Kristoforov. The lovers are only reunited for a moment before she dies and he commits suicide. It was in a way a portent of Yavorov's own end four years later.

A second drama, *When the Thunder Strikes* (1911), shows

the frightful consequences of an old lie in the lives of the next generation. Whether Yavorov would have developed into a great dramatist is perhaps uncertain since his career was cut short by his suicide. Yet he has remained one of the leading members of his group and one of the greatest lyric poets of Bulgaria.

The third of the outstanding authors of this group was Petko Todorov who was born in Elena in 1879. His father was conservative and well-to-do. He had a considerable library of Bulgarian, Russian, French and Turkish books so that the young Todorov had every opportunity to see the good side of the old Bulgarian way of life. After some time in the gymnasium of Tirnovo, he transferred to France and studied in Toulouse where he learned to know the modern French writers and also French translations of such authors as Ibsen, Strindberg and Hauptmann, all of whom were to have an influence on his writings. After a passing infatuation with the writings of Marx and Engels, he returned to Bulgaria in 1897 and was arrested at Ruse but was soon released. He then returned to western Europe and studied at the University of Berne in Switzerland and then in Berlin. In 1898 he returned to Sofia and secured a position in the Bulgarian National Library, working on a doctoral dissertation on "The Relationship of the Slavs to Bulgarian Literature," a subject which led him to visit Prague and Lviv where he became friendly with Ukrainian writers like Ivan Franko, Olha Kobylyanska and the other friends of Lesya Ukrainka. He stayed in the Bulgarian National Library most of his life, but he became gravely ill and died in Switzerland in 1916 during World War I. After the war in 1921, his body was returned to Sofia.

Petko Todorov began his career under the influence of socialistic thought with poems and stories on the themes approved by the socialist thought of the day, and he met with some success. Yet his heart was not in the social struggle or with the development of Populism in Bulgaria. By the time that he returned from his second trip to Europe and his stay in Germany, he had wholeheartedly adopted the ideas of the modern Symbolist movement, and it was in that vein that he continued until his death. The influence of Ibsen and Hauptmann was clearly marked and so too was that of Lesya Ukrainka, whom he had met during her visits in Bulgaria with her uncle and cousins, the Shishmanovs. Like her, he endeavored to acclimate in Bulgarian literature the newer and more modern philosophy of literature and to broaden the scope of the native conceptions without abandoning the national wealth of folklore and tradition.

His best work was perhaps his *Idyls,* short prose minatures illustrating some phase of life, some emotion often expressed in symbolist form, and incorporating very frequently the thought of Nietzsche and the superman only to unveil it as a mask for emptiness and superficiality. All of the characters search for happiness, but they can never find it because they are always looking for it in the wrong place. Thus we have the *Bear-Tamer.* In this story the young Kalina falls in love with a gypsy bear-tamer. Despite the protests of her friends, she goes off with him and marries in gypsy fashion. She has to stay with him as he wanders around; she is forced to sell her jewels in the Dobrudja as the bear-tamer leads his wandering life, while her mother pines away in longing for her daughter's return. There is something of this sadness and frustration in all of the *Idyls.* Either a man seeks for solitude and then too late discovers that he wants a home or he secures a home and finds that he needs solitude.

Pencho Slaveykov early pointed out to him the richness of the Bulgarian tradition, and Todorov in his sketches and in his dramas develops native themes. However, he does not do this in the same way as the mass of the older Bulgarian writers. He tries to put into his themes some individual meaning, some personal touch, some aspect of human psychology which all too often makes his writings seem remote from the spirit of the average Bulgarian.

Again and again he retells some story of tradition in a symbolist setting. Thus in *The Builders* he revives the old legend of the immuring of a maiden within the walls of a newly constructed building to increase the security of the building, but he gives it a novel turn. The peasants are building a church. When its success is menaced by the discord of the villagers and the threat of an attack by Turkish robbers, Khristo, a poor peasant but the beloved of the village beauty Rada, leads the peasants against the bandits. His rival, Doncho, remains behind and is induced by the superstitious to take an oath that the first girl to enter the church building will be killed by the falling of a scaffold. By trickery he brings Rada to the spot, claiming that Khristo is inside, mortally wounded. Then he repents but it is too late. Rada is killed. Khristo and his men return victorious, but they curse the church. Khristo leaves the village, while Doncho commits suicide.

The *Samodiva* (The Fairy) is again drawn from folklore as Lesya Ukrainka later drew in Ukrainian *The Forest Song* and Hauptmann, *The Sunken Bell*. The young Stiliyan, a lover of the mountains and freedom, falls in love with a mountain fairy. She loves him in return but no sooner has she assumed human form and adopted the humdrum life of the village than he becomes bored and gloomy and unloving. A neighbor, Boyko, revives in her the image of that Stiliyan whom she has loved in the mountains and together with him she leaves the venomous house of her husband for another form of free life. It is the same message of the impossibility of adapting beauty to the sordid realism of every day life that we find in Hauptmann's *The Sunken Bell* and other European plays of the same period.

It is a question how well Todorov has succeeded in breathing new wine into old bottles of folklore and tradition. His efforts are often artistically successful. However, he often produced something that does not seem native to the Bulgarian soil and the Bulgarian character, even though he clothed it in a superb Bulgarian setting. There is more of the artificial in him than in Yavorov, but for the European who desires to find European motifs in Bulgarian literature, Todorov stands without peer. It is only to be regretted that he died before he had worked out a final synthesis of his subject matter and his methods.

A somewhat less important, but perhaps more popular, writer who may be assigned to this group is Kiril Khristov. He was born in 1875 in Stara Zagora. After the early death of his parents he was brought up by various relatives until he went to Italy to study navigation. Ill health kept him from continuing in this field, and he returned to Bulgaria as a teacher and finally a university professor. After World War I he again left Bulgaria to wander around Germany and Czechoslovakia in a self-imposed exile until his death in 1944.

Khristov early made his mark as an erotic and Anacreontic poet. He was, nevertheless, not without deeper motifs and a remarkable gift for language that made him popular from the time his earliest works appeared. His first poems seemed to place him among the Modernists, and he was welcomed by the more serious classes of Bulgarian society. As time passed, however, he sank into a less ambitious role. His early inventions in the field of the personal lyric were far outstripped by Pencho Slaveykov and his friends. Yet, Khristov never lost his popularity, and he worked in all branches of poetry. In fact his poetical drama *Boyan Magesnikut* (Boyan the Magician), which appeared in 1911, was the first verse drama in Bulgarian. It was a patriotic tale of the defence of Bulgaria against the agents of Byzantium. His collections of patriotic songs were well received, and on the whole, without being a star of the first magnitude, Khristov was a symbol of the heights to which Bulgarian literature had developed before World War I.

By the time of the Balkan Wars and World War I, the poets of the day had in fact revolutionized the older Bulgarian literature. They had introduced the new European poetry with all of its Western and Russian characteristics, and Bulgaria seemed ready to move ahead. Then began the series of tragedies that were to color the next years.

CHAPTER NINE

Bulgarian Prose and Drama

During the last decade of the nineteenth century and the first of the twentieth, Bulgarian prose and the Bulgarian stage did not pass through such a revolutionary development as did the poetry. There are several reasons for this. The tradition of prose literature had been firmly established even before the liberation by Karavelov, and afterwards by Vazov, in a Populist and a peasant tradition and as a study especially of the life of the peasants before and immediately after the liberation. Furthermore, many of the old masters who had established and developed this tradition lived on and worked fruitfully until well after World War I, and they never lost their hold upon the reading public. Thus there was little or no call for the appearance of a new set of writers with new principles and new themes. In lesser degree this was also true of the Bulgarian stage and of the first phases of the development of the Bulgarian National Theatre which was founded in 1907.

The outstanding innovator was in a way Georgi Stamatov. He was born in 1869 in Tiraspol, Government of Kherson in Ukraine in the Russian Empire. His father, a lawyer, had left Bulgaria before the liberation, and it was not until 1879 that he returned to his country and became President of the Court of Cassation. His son until then had been brought up as a Russian. He had attended Russian schools and apparently did not know the Bulgarian language or even realize that he was not a pure-blooded Russian. In 1882 the young Stamatov returned to Bulgaria as a boy of fourteen to have his first experience of life in his father's country. He entered the military school and became an officer in the Bulgarian army, but, disliking the discipline and routine of army life, he resigned and studied law.

He soon became a judge, but before long he retired and henceforth lived in Sofia and devoted himself to literature until his death in 1942.

In his early youth he had naturally become acquainted with the classics of Russian literature, especially Pushkin and Lermontov. He was also an ardent reader of Byron and Heine. His knowledge of these writers induced him to become a poet, and he published one poem in 1890. However, he soon shifted his interest to prose, an area in which he was also familiar with the works of the Russian writers of the nineteenth century. He published his first story, *Why the Zagorovs are Happy in Thought,* in 1893, and from that time he gave up all thoughts of poetry and concentrated on prose works, which appeared in all of the leading Bulgarian periodicals. In 1905 he published a collected volume of some of his works, a small volume of *Sketches* in 1915. In 1929 he planned to reissue a complete collection of his stories, but he failed to carry out his design.

Unlike most of the Bulgarian prose writers, Stamatov dealt almost exclusively with the urban population, especially of the smaller cities which he knew from his service as a judge. *Sande Klicharski* typifies Stamatov's method of description, as he pictures the galling monotony of the sleepy little city which gradually, with its seductive calm, poisons even the most strenuous and the most ambitious. The story depicts a judge, Sande Klicharski, who is so overwhelmed by his environment that he has on his table no pencil or ink, no books, merely a pitcher of water, a comb, and a brush for his clothes. It is a picture of spiritual desolation made worse by the fact that the victim is completely unaware of his intellectual disintegration.

In the same way Stamatov studies the development of Sofia. His stories reveal the many-faceted life of the city from the time of the liberation and its growth from a quiet town to a great city, the capital of the country. Many of his stories deal with the artistic life of the capital with artists as the main characters. It is a curious fact that in a large number of his stories the name is taken from the leading character, man or woman, whose life is twisted out of its expected course by the force of circumstances.

Stamatov is profoundly pessimistic as well as amoralistic in his depiction of his characters, for he takes an almost malicious joy in describing the sins and the frailties of his heroes. This attitude is especially marked in the treatment of his women, who cannot seem to accept the bounds that life has imposed upon them, whether in marriage or the family, and seek new fields in which they can dabble. But always his leading figure is an active and powerful individual, yearning for the satisfaction of some ideal and only too willing to talk about it at length, like Stamatov himself. Still, his distinguishing feature is his knowledge of the human heart which he analyzes in a few deft strokes.

Stamatov was much influenced by the methods of the great Russian prose writers, whom he knew thoroughly. He was also influenced by the French, especially Flaubert, Balzac and Zola. He introduced Naturalism into Bulgarian literature and, like Zola, he stopped at no detail to lay bare the psychological motives of his characters. He is still the great Bulgarian delineator of urban life. None of his predecessors or successors has known so thoroughly this subject which profoundly interested him. He illustrates all aspects of life and all classes of the city population from the stupid and repulsive bureaucrats to the idealistic artists, people in all degrees of wealth and poverty, but always he looks for and finds the secret spring which gives the keynote to their reason for existence and their being what they are. It is small wonder that with his intensive preoccupation with psychology, Stamatov never became a really popular author. He was too far removed from the general run of the literature and from that lyric touch that made Vazov's stories so successful.

In this he is very different from the other leading prose writer of the same period, Elin Pelin, who primarily pictured the older Bulgarian village life and its disintegration under the impact of the modern changes. Elin Pelin (his real name was Dimitar Ivanov) was born in the village of Saylovo, region of Sofia, in 1878. He left the gymnasium in the fifth class to become a teacher in a country school in a small village, the type of existence which he had always loved and admired and from which he drew his inspiration. He later tried to complete his education but could not pass the sixth grade. He was rejected for the Art Academy and so remained a teacher and writer. He spent his life defending the populism of the Bulgarian Teachers' Association and reflecting the thoughts and aims of those idealists who went into the villages and bore without complaint the hardships and miseries of the life of a country teacher in an almost uneducated community. He died, respected and admired, in 1949.

For these teachers he published for some time a quasi-periodical, *The Village Conversation,* for which he wrote most of the articles himself. He was finally obliged to abandon the publication because of the lack of subscribers. He published many of his best stories in this periodical. He issued his early works under his own name, but in 1898 he published a poem signed with the name Elin Pelin. This poem, on the death of Levski, appeared in the *Memorial Volume* on the twenty-fifth anniversary of Levski's death. From this time on he used the pen-name consistently.

In 1904 he published a volume of his collected works and in 1906 a second volume. During this period he also brought out *Ashes of My Cigar,* a small volume of whimsical poems and grotesques, and he followed this with *Ashes of My Cigarette,* a collection of similar whimsical stories and poems. In his collection of 1906 he included several stories and poems that show the influence of Nekrasov and Yavorov and also an excellent translation of Edgar Allen Poe's *Raven.*

Thus Elin Pelin succeeded in combining many of the best features of the older Bulgarian prose with a touch of symbolism and of the newer techniques which were being introduced into the contemporary poetry.

His next collection, *A Bouquet for a Hero,* came during the period of World War I. This consists of a series of war stories, but, again, Elin Pelin did not resort either to condemnation or praise of war. He maintained his own ideals and used his pen for the consolation of his fellow citizens. Through it all he remained a pure artist, but one with a deep feeling for the needs of his people. He differed from many of the older writers who allowed their indignation and feeling for social justice to get the better of them and who chose all their themes from the baser side of human nature.

Another important part of his work was his writings for children, and he published many poems and stories attuned to a child's mind and range of interests. In his time he was supreme in this field, and his works for children have become classics in Bulgarian.

In 1928, after years of silence, he published still another collection, *Black Rose*. The very title was symbolic of eternity. Externally the volume seemed to show the influence of Baudelaire and Poe, but behind this exterior there is the definite portrait of Elin Pelin himself with his high regard for humanity, his whimsical moods and his deep knowledge of the thoughts and reactions of the Bulgarian peasant.

In his story, *The Earth,* he traces the influence of the land upon Bulgarian psychology. A rich *chorbadji,* Enyo Kunshin, in his quest for land and money abandons his first love to marry a rich girl. Then he wants his brother's inheritance, and when Ivan refuses to hand it over, he tries to kill him but only succeeds in making him deaf and dumb. The crime is never discovered, but it preys upon Enyo's mind. He turns to drink, loses all his property, and finally dies a miserable death in the home of his first love who has forgiven him and in her happiness with her husband takes pity on the poor wretch. After his death, his body is left in the church with a lighted candle in his dead hands. This candle falls over and burns his entire body. This is a symbolist tale, but the emphasis, as in all of Elin Pelin's work, is not on the social problems involved but on the psychological development of his characters, an element not stressed in the older authors.

Elin Pelin realized as did few of the writers of his day that conditions in Bulgaria were rapidly changing. Education was penetrating the villages and the old patriarchal order was passing. There were new methods of production, new wants of the villagers to be supplied, new responsibilities for them to assume. He considered it his task to picture the psychology of those changes without touching upon the general questions concerning whether the changes were being effected in the best possible way or were for better or worse. As a result although he superficially continued the old tradition of village tales, in reality, he introduced many new notes into the literature, notes drawn from the modern writers of the world but passed through the prism of his own spirit, which adapted them to the Bulgarian mind and heart.

His best work, like that of most of his generation, was done before the period of storm and stress which opened with the Balkan Wars of 1912. His character and style were already formed, and he proceeded during the post-war period to develop his qualities still further without adding significant changes or allowing his spirit to be dulled by the adverse conditions around him.

Bulgarian drama passed through the same stages of development, as the amateur groups in the various important cities gradually became more and more professional and able to handle not only the plays based on the local scenes and traditions but also the masterpieces of world drama. In 1904 Ivan Shishmanov, as Minister of Education, took the first steps for the formation of a National Theatre. The theatre was opened January 3, 1907 with a special play written for it by Vazov and the performance of one act of Drumev's *Ivanku*.

This was symptomatic of the course of the Bulgarian drama. The historical plays of the early writers and their comedies based upon amusing examples of corruption and ignorance in village life were summed up and developed by Vazov, who was and remained the most popular of the dramatic writers. Yet this style degenerated all too often into melodrama or into saccharine performances like those of Evgeniya Mars (1878-1945), which were popular in their day.

A little later the dramatists began to feel the influences of Ibsen and the newer psychological drama which sought to present more complicated situations and to explain the psychological motives that urged individuals to step off the beaten track even at the risk of producing their own downfall and unhappiness. Among the authors of this period was Ivan Kirikov (1878-1936). Thus in *The Lark* (1906) the sober young botanist Strymnev is led, against the advice of his solid wife and everyone else, by a young, adventurous and aspiring student, Danila, to attempt the ascent of a mountain so as to rise to the heights of ecstasy. The couple are overwhelmed in a mountain storm and while Strymnev succeeds in rescuing his friend, Danila, she dies in a monastery from her experiences and he resumes his earthbound but respectable and normal existence.

Another writer of this group is Ana Karima (1872-1948), the wife of one of the liberal socialist leaders of the day. In her drama, *Awakening* (1902), she pictures a young and ambitious woman trying to get out of the rut in which life has placed her. Yet, unable to leave because of her love for her young daughter, she remains in an environment which she despises but which she still feels a certain satisfaction in keeping.

From this period we can see the gradual development of that style of Modernistic thinking which was introduced by Pencho Slaveykov and developed by Yavorov and Todorov with their tendencies to oppose the artist to the crowd which has little appreciation of the artistic or psychological needs of the able individual. This was an idea that had become familiar during the preceding decades in the countries of western Europe and in Russia, but it was a novelty for the Bulgarian peasants, who had long realized the problem but had never put it into words under the pressure of the needs of the liberation and the difficulties of establishing the new independent state.

Thus step by step in every form of literature the ideas and ideals of European literature began to penetrate into Bulgarian reality. By 1914 the process had definitely triumphed, and Bulgarian literature in all its forms was ready to participate actively in the general development of European literature as an equal. Then there commenced the period of disaster, which seriously checked the national development and warped it in many ways.

CHAPTER TEN

The Period of Discouragement

Bulgarian hopes for union with a free Macedonia grew even higher in 1912. In that year the country made an alliance with Serbia, Greece and Montenegro for the First Balkan War against the Ottoman Empire. By previous agreement, in case of Turkish defeat, Bulgaria was to receive a liberated Macedonia as part of her territory. The war was successful and the allied powers won all their objectives including the city of Odrin up to the Chataldja lines near Constantinople. Then the rivalry between the Great Powers (the Triple Alliance of Germany, Austria-Hungary and Italy, and the Triple Entente of Great Britain, France and Russia) for the control of the Balkans was renewed. The Great Powers agreed on the creation of an independent Albania at the expense of Serbia and Greece. These countries to recompense themselves made further demands on Bulgaria.

As a result, in 1913 the Second Balkan War broke out. In this war Bulgaria was opposed by all her former allies and also by Turkey and Romania. Bulgaria, defeated, was not only deprived of the fruits of her victories in the First Balkan War but was also compelled to cede to Romania the Southern Dobrudja, which she had held since 1878.

While the country was smarting over this defeat, World War I commenced between the two coalitions of Great Powers. Because of her geopolitical location Bulgaria found herself in a tragic position. The war aims of the two alliances favored the involvement of Bulgaria in the penultimate phase of European imperialism. Germany, the actual leader of the Triple Alliance, elaborated the idea of *Mitteleuropa* along with a plan for building a railroad directly from Berlin to Bagdad and the Persian

130

Gulf. This would have created for her a direct commercial route by land to the Asian market and eliminated the effects of the British control of Gibraltar and Suez. Bulgaria was on the direct route of this railroad and Germany made glowing promises to her for her support and held out the prospect of a great market for her agricultural products.

On the other hand the Triple Entente considered Bulgaria as the stepping stone and key for the entrance of Russia into Constantinople. One group of Bulgarian politicians strongly favored alliance with the Entente, but the liberals remembered their previous experiences with Russia and feared that the victory of Russia would mean the end of Bulgarian independence. In addition to this Russian support had been given so generously to Serbia and Montenegro that the Bulgarians saw themselves endangering all their major interests by the support of Russia. Also the Entente policy toward Greece was at least problematical. It was therefore not too difficult for Tsar Ferdinand to push Bulgaria into the war on the side of the Triple Alliance, once neutrality became very difficult.

By 1918 the growing power of the Triple Entente, aided by the United States, despite the Russian collapse began to create doubts of ultimate German victory in the minds of the Bulgarians. When in the last phase of the war the Anglo-French troops broke the Bulgarian-German lines north of Salonika, Bulgaria sued for peace. Riots broke out all over the country. Tsar Ferdinand was compelled to abdicate in favor of his son Boris III, and after a short period when the Bulgarian malcontents tried to establish a republic, an Agrarian cabinet was formed under the rule of Tsar Boris.

The leader of the Agrarians, Alexander Stamboliyski, was the idol of the peasants and a strong supporter of peasant rule. In fact he was the founder of the Green International, the organization of the peasants of all the central and east European countries. To strengthen himself, however, he accepted the help of the small urban Bulgarian Communist group, the extreme Marxists who had passed under the influence of Lenin after the October Revolution of 1917. Many of Stamboliyski's measures in the agrarian sphere and his efforts to establish good relations between Bulgaria and her neighbors displeased the conservative and military classes. His efforts at administration also annoyed many of the intellectual groups, who felt that he did not give them enough influence and subjected them to galling restrictions. On June 8 and 9, 1923 his government was overthrown by a military-reactionary group, and Stamboliyski was killed. A new conservative government was set up under Prof. A. Tsankov, and a conservative reign of terror started. Tsar Boris finally succeeded in putting an end to what was almost civil war. Tsankov resigned and a new conservative government, less extreme, took its place. Order was gradually restored, although among the peasants there continued much hidden opposition, which the Communists tried in every way to fan into open struggle. Cabinets were made and fell without any reason, and finally in 1934 Tsar Boris adopted an authoritarian policy dubbed by his opponents as fascist, since the Tsar had married an Italian princess who was the granddaughter of King Nicholas of Montenegro. Yet, although powerless, the dissolved political parties continued to have their almost open machinery, and their leaders were represented in the more or less handpicked National Assembly. It was against this background that the Bulgarian writers after World War I were compelled to work and function, in an era of national discouragement and pessimism which had replaced the glowing optimism of the pre-war years.

Most of the men who now began to make their reputations had been born in the eighteen eighties and nineties. Some of them had begun to write before the First Balkan War, but all of them achieved their fullness of reputation only in the period after the war and during or after the civil disturbances. They were young enough when these disturbances began, to reflect the various moods of the Bulgarian people, each in his own way.

The exception is perhaps the greatest of modern Bulgarian lyric poets, Dimcho Debelyanov. Like the poet Michael Lermontov in Russian literature, he finished his life's course before the men of his own generation were fully mature. The fifty poems which he left in his short life have been applauded and acclaimed since by all sections of Bulgarian thought, including the Communists, although they have shown some hesitation about it.

Debelyanov was born in 1887 in Koprivshtitsa of a ruined family. He was left an orphan at the age of nine but somehow he got an education in Plovdiv and Sofia. He was compelled to make a living as best he could as translator, proofreader, and official of the lower grades. He was always without funds and lived under the most adverse conditions. He took part in the Balkan and World Wars, and he was finally killed in battle in 1916 at the age of twenty-nine. It was one of the saddest moments for Bulgarian literature when this promising poet was removed from the scene, but he had already produced enough so that his reputation after his death continued to grow.

It is easy to call Debelyanov a Symbolist, for that term had come into favor in Bulgaria through the later works of Yavorov and Todorov. However, Debelyanov was more than that for he was a natural lyric poet with only the philosophy that came from a full realization of his own talent. It is true that he wrote a few poems criticizing the policy of the Tsar, but they were only incidental to the zeal and energy which he poured out in his reflections on his own life and aspirations. To him beauty was everything, a beauty which involved not only the things of the spirit but the things of the flesh. Debelyanov was hungry for life, life in all its varied manifestations, whether in wine, women or thought. It gave his poetry a fullness, a richness, and a sincerity that those poets could not have who worked out their ideals and their methods by thought and careful effort. Debelyanov threw himself into the act of living, and his natural talents did the rest. It is easy to say that under the conditions of his life there could have been no good outcome for him, if he had lived. He knew the sufferings of his people, he knew the hardships of war, he did not thrill only to patriotic slogans but poured out exactly his own feelings, his own desires, and he did it so exquisitely as a real poet that he achieved in the few years of his life a genuine immortality. Perceiving the evil of the world around him, he drew from it not a feeling of despair but a consciousness of his own spiritual capacity which led him to an unmystical mysticism as to the essence of life and an assertion of his own will to live.

Debelyanov died before the new generation was fairly developed. This generation, largely in the name of Symbolism, developed a phenomenon previously almost unknown in Bulgaria, the growth of literary groups gathered around some literary journal and guided by certain critics and theoreticians. There were three of these that flourished in the twenties. The oldest was the *Zlatorog* group (the Golden Horn), clustered around a journal of that name and guided by Vladimir Vasilev and Professor Boyan Penev. This group placed great emphasis on the technical form of literary works and aimed to continue the tradition of Pencho Slaveykov and Yavorov.

The second group was *Hyperion,* which was started somewhat later. Its leading critic was Bojan Angelov, and its great exponent and editor was the symbolist poet Todor Trayanov. At first this group tried to express still more forcefully than the *Zlatorog* the progressive movements in Bulgarian literature, but later it broadened its field as some of its members gradually changed their artistic position quite definitely and some of them, such as Lyudmil Stoyanov, drifted toward leftist ideas in politics.

Another schism from the *Zlatorog* group was that of the writer and critic Konstantin Galabov and Chavdar Mutafov. Both of these men having studied extensively in Germany, they attempted to introduce into literature a form of post-war German Expressionism. They broke away and formed their own group, *Strelets* (The Archer), and their example was followed on the eve of World War II by still other associations, each of them meeting in its own special coffee house or restaurant. All of these, like similar formations in France and the other Slavic countries, found it necessary to initiate their proceedings with a series of formal literary *credos* and statements of artistic principles which were very alien to the more artless, even if talented, critics of the period before the Balkan Wars.

Side by side with this division into schools came two other phenomena which were characteristic of the development of Bulgarian Symbolism in its various degrees. The first of these was preoccupation with mysticism which had been singularly lacking in the Bulgarian writers of the period before the Balkan Wars. In Bulgaria it tended to take the form of an interest in the ancient *Bogomils,* that heretical, anti-governmental sect of the early centuries which was, at least in some of its forms, severely dualistic. Their outstanding modern exponent was Ivan Grozev (b. 1872), an otherwise undistinguished writer. He wrote and produced in 1922 in the Bulgarian National Theatre a play, *The Golden Cup,* which extolled the virtue of the Bogomils and their spiritual doctrines as opposed to the coldly formal patriarch and the corrupt emperor of the Byzantine court, probably Alexis Komnenos, in the twelfth century. Here the Bulgarian Bogomil leader resists the power of the evil spirit, Satanail, and finally, at the moment of his execution, slays by mystical power the corrupt emperor, while the people remain silent as at the end of Pushkin's *Boris Godunov.* The play was an appeal to the national traditions, but the methods used were those of a mystic and believer in mysticism.

We can see in this same work another important feature which had already appeared in the later works of Vazov: a stress upon the past, upon Bulgarian history, especially the history of the First Bulgarian Empire. This was a trend that was greatly overemphasized in the late thirties, when for a few years Bulgarian literature almost turned into a glorification of the past and of the former Bulgarian rule in those territories which the modern Bulgarians claimed for their own. This overgrown and overstressed sense of history was one of the great factors that led Bulgaria again in World War II to ally itself with the Axis powers without considering the possibility that such a policy might lead to another disaster.

Undoubtedly the outstanding Symbolist of this period was Nikolay Liliyev (b. 1886 in Stara Zagora). He studied in the Commercial School in Svishtov, and from there he received a scholarship to Paris. After teaching in the commercial schools of Sofia and Svishtov, he was sent to Vienna and Munich. For a while he worked in the National Theatre and later returned to the commercial gymnasium in Varna, but his heart was always in Paris. Yet even in Paris he was unable to identify himself with the life around him. Night and solitude were his favorite themes, as we can see from two collections of poems, *Birds in the Night* and *Spots of Moonlight.* His verse is delicate and refined, but while he had a great influence upon later poets, he did not have the robustness or clarity that attracted readers. He was a poet's poet in a narrower sense than any of his predecessors.

Todor Trayanov, who was born in T. Pazardjik in 1882, studied in Sofia and then in Austria and Germany. He began to write before the Balkan Wars but he found himself in his *Bulgarian Ballads* (1921) and later in *Romantic Ballads* and *The Freed Man,* and others of his mature works. As editor of *Hyperion* he had the opportunity to display his gifts of imagery and of phraseology but again, as in the case of Liliyev, his works had little essential personality. They are far too often mere collections of beautiful phrases, although they are perhaps more comprehensible and clear than are those of Liliyev. There is in many of them a mistiness and a lack of clarity which have not been characteristic of the Bulgarians, and although Trayanov is clearly a master, the number of his poems on which his immortality can depend is rather limited. He died in 1944.

In this period, too, we find that women began to play an important role in Bulgarian literature. One of these was Dora Gabe born in Dobrych in 1886 and reared in the Dobrudja which Bulgaria lost in 1913. After studying in Varna and then in Geneva and Grenoble, she returned to Bulgaria. She published her first collection, *Violets,* in 1908 and then in 1928 *The Way of the Earth,* which contains her mature work. The latter is far removed from the mild romanticism of *The Violets* which came out in the happy days before the disturbances. It reflects her disillusionment with the world and the general course of events, including her own fate. However, it is deeply poetic, and Dora Gabe can well claim to be one of the leading poets of the *Zlatorog* group. In addition to her poetry she published a series of sketches on her life in the Dobrudja, and she has been one of the most prolific writers of children's literature on a high plane.

Still another poetess of high literary rank is Elisaveta Bagryana, who was born in Sliven and commenced to publish only in 1919. Her first collection, *The Eternal and the Holy,* which appeared in 1927, and *The Star of the Sailor* (1931) reveal her deeply sensitive nature which had survived the difficulties that she had during the height of the troubles when she was expelled from her position in the government service because of the journals to which she had been contributing. Later she joined the *Zlatorog* group, and her real literary ability was recognized.

A third poetess of high merit was Mara Belcheva, who has maintained her independence and has published several collections of poems marked by a deep spirit of philosophical resignation.

Another member of *Zlatorog* who developed an original, even if unclear, style was Nikolay Raynov. He was born in Tirnovo in 1888 and after studying abroad became a professor of the History of Art in the Art Academy. This had a marked effect upon his work, for he published many articles and books in his special field. At times he wrote such verse as *The Bogomil Legends* which appeared in 1912. Practically all his writings, in verse or prose, reflect his deep absorption in the past of Bulgaria, which is evident in such works as *Visions from Old Bulgaria* (1918) and *The Book of the Tsars* (1918). Soon after writing these, he turned his eyes to the East as in *The Eyes of Arabia.* Everywhere he invokes the past with a mystical fervor and treats his subjects in a symbolistic or a naturalistic manner. His treatment of love varies from a mystical admiration for its spiritual quality to an equally mystical presentation of its most fleshly aspects. Yet, despite all of his variations, it is hard to know what Raynov really thinks. He cloaks his thought under a mass of symbols, and his fertile pen conceals the essence of that reality which he avoids preaching in clear language.

Another writer of especial interest is Georgi Raichev, who was born in 1882 in the region of Stara Zagora where he received the bulk of his education. Raichev early commenced to write poetry, but he abandoned this for prose. He published his first story, *Travellers,* in the journal of Strashimirov. After World War I he transferred to the *Zlatorog* group and became one of its foremost representatives. In 1918 he published two autobiographical stories, *The Little World* and *Tsaritsa Neranza.* Later he edited a volume called simply *Stories* (1923). This was followed by *The Song of the Mountain* (1928) and *Legends of the Tsars* (1931). In all of these Raichev showed that he was primarily interested in the psychology of individuals who were almost pathological in their actions. He seeks for unusual features in their lives and tries to explain them in psychological terms. At his best, as in *The Sin,* he has produced the best psychological literature in modern Bulgaria. In his most successful stories, although he has stressed the pathological elements, he has shown real sympathy and understanding in his analysis of his characters.

Undoubtedly the most talented prose writer of this period was Iordan Iovkov, who was born in 1884 in the village of Jeravna and brought up in the Dobrudja on the border between Bulgaria and Romania. He completed the gymnasium in Sofia and then for some years taught in the village schools of the Dobrudja, where he learned to know all the details of the life of the people and worked out his own philosophy of literature. Iovkov stands clearly in the tradition of village literature, but, having no political axe to grind, he went beyond this as it had been practiced previously. That was the chief feature of his two volumes called *War Stories* and five volumes, *Prose Tales,* as well as his three dramas. No Bulgarian writer on the village has been so able to maintain an artistic calm in his description of the peasants. Iovkov tries to understand without condemning, and in stories like *Ivan Belin* he describes the peasant shepherd who has lived his life in the open, far from humanity, and has never learned to hate, even when wrong is done to him. It is this lack of moral judgment that separates Iovkov from most of his contemporaries. Whether he is describing the reactions of the Bulgarian soldier in war time or the life of the unfortunate peasant, he looks at his subject with the calm certainty that the qualities of man are universal and that every man has not only his good but his weak side. He tries to stress neither. He merely pictures all aspects in admirable prose. His refusal to make judgments has won the dislike of all those classes of the population which, each in its own way, have tried to bend literature to a social and political program. Such a program meant nothing to Iovkov, and he paid as little attention to one as to another of them. He contented himself with being what he was, a pure artist not losing himself in his enthusiasms but observing and understanding what goes on in the minds and hearts of his characters. When he died in 1937, he left a heritage to Bulgarian literature which was almost universally admired by all those readers and critics who placed good writing and human sympathy higher than efforts to reform humanity in one way or another. He possessed in high degree that feature, common to the greatest artists, of viewing life warmly, impartially, and sympathetically in all its manifestations.

A writer of a quite unusual type was Dimitar Shishmanov, the son of Professor Ivan S. Shishmanov and the grandson of the Ukrainian professor in Sofia, Mykhaylo Drahomaniv. He was born in Sofia in 1889 and received the education that we would expect for a son of an intellectual family. Following his graduation in law from the University of Geneva, he occupied a large number of responsible political posts. For a while after World War I he was in charge of the Commission on Reparations. After passing through various ministries, he was, on the eve of World War II, Bulgarian Minister in Athens, a very difficult post but one which he filled to the general satisfaction of both the Bulgarians and the Greeks. At the end of World War II he was sufficiently prominent to be singled out for the vengeance of the Communists as an outstanding conservative. He was accordingly executed along with the leaders who had led Bulgaria into the war and then sought cooperation with the Western powers.

He began to write before World War I but he had a marked outburst of productivity after the War when in quick succession he published *High Life* (1920), *Deputy Stoyanov* (1920), and *The Rebel* (1921), long novels in which he sought to work out the psychological basis for the three important features of the Bulgarian life of the day, sententiousness, bureaucracy and bribery. There was a pause in his literary work, and then in 1924 he issued *A Strange Band* and even later a drama, *The Nightmare* (1929). In these later works, unlike the first series, he depicted unusual and odd characters, whom he tried to understand in all the manifold ramifications of their being. He also tried to assimilate and explain in Bulgarian the most diverse features of modern European life. His keen and often whimsical character was shown again on the eve of World War II in his handling of the Greeks in *Shadows on the Acropolis,* one of the best tributes to the Greek genius in any language, with only one story that might be construed as favoring the Bulgarian side of the argument. In this highly whimsical series of sketches, he pictures the Wandering Jew Ahasver (Ahasuerus) as a young man with a weary and aged soul wandering around Athens and pointing out the crudities of the modern world and their corresponding features in antiquity. Thus the narrator is shocked by the floodlights on the Parthenon, only to have Ahasuerus bring up Phidias to explain that he had attempted the same thing with huge bonfires, but it was not so successful or brilliant. So, point by point, Ahasuerus makes his argument that the new is but an extension of the old in both its virtues and vices and can be interpreted in the same terms as antiquity. Shishmanov carried this attitude into his critical work, both in literature and music, with the same readiness to defend the new when it was proceeding on rational and practicable lines. It was this same regard for the achievements of European culture as a whole that guided him in his political and diplomatic activity and led, under Communism, to his untimely death. In a sense he was the best product of the highest traditions and types of Bulgarian culture in its full development as a part of the European world.

The leading novelist of this period was Dobri Nemirov who was born in Ruse in 1882 and commenced to write on the eve of World War I. His first stories were halting as if he were not sure exactly what he wished to depict, but he had faith in himself and his own powers and step by step he proceeded to master his theme: the development of Bulgaria during his own lifetime. Year by year he published new novels which met with wider and wider favor. Some of them, like *The Brothers,* show the conflicts in the Bulgarian village immediately after the liberation. In others he brought this same subject up to date and described the confusion and the doubts that possessed many of his contemporaries. He explored the same themes, but not so successfully, in his plays, which had the same solid virtues as his novels: an understanding of the Bulgarian mind and the Bulgarian situation and a capacity for expressing his results in clear and fluent Bulgarian. Then in the thirties he, too, yielded to the historical movement and in *The Angel-Voiced Singer* he pictured a young and innocent Bulgarian with a wonderful voice at the corrupt court of the Komneni emperors in Constantinople and contrasted the manners of the Bulgarians with those of the Byzantines to the disadvantage of the latter. His personality corresponded to his work, for he was a sincere and unassuming individual who was fully conscious of what he was trying to accomplish for his people. He was in a way the best continuator of the traditions of Vazov, although it was a Vazov brought up to date and able to see the modern point of view and the modern problems. He died in 1945 in Sofia.

Another writer who understood and tried to explain the bloody events of the post-World War I period was Konstantin Konstantinov who was born in Sliven in 1890. He studied law in Sofia and later became a judge and an adviser to the State Bank. He accompanied this career with literary work and published a number of stories and novels such as *Blood* (1933), in which he brought out the distinctive features of the attempted revolutionary movements after World War I and also the ideological bases behind them. He pictured the dying provincial cities after World War I under the stress and strain of the civil disturbances, and the influence of love encouraging a man to conquer or to die. Konstantinov expressed his message without resorting to the petty devices of propaganda or injecting his own ideas so as to tip the balance. A relatively minor author, he is still a credit and more to the causes in which he believed and which he served.

Another man who deserves more than passing mention is S. L. Kostov (1880-1939). Born in Sofia and educated both in Sofia and Vienna, he later became the director of the Ethnological Museum in Sofia for which he published many excellent works on the Bulgarian national costume. Yet, he is known in literature primarily for his comedies which were among the most popular pieces in the repertoire of the Bulgarian National Theatre. Kostov was a natural comedian and his serious dramas did not harmonize with his whimsical temperament. His best plays were *The Gold Mine* and *Golemanov*. In the first of these he satirizes the greed for wealth of certain individuals like the retired public servant, Khadjiyev, who risks his entire savings in buying his way into a gold mine. He has been swindled by conscienceless rascals who have salted the mine, but he is so convinced that a fortune is his that he ruins his entire career and makes himself thoroughly ridiculous. *Golemanov* is on the same general theme, but here the hero is a prominent deputy who stops at no risks or chicanery to secure for himself a post as a Minister with all the prerequisites that such a post provides. In both of these plays Kostov made fun of many of the accepted features of Bulgarian life after World War I. He created synthetic personalities drawn from his own experiences with the great and the near-great of Sofia. Although he undoubtedly had certain individuals as his models, no one could be offended when he pointed out the vices of which they themselves were fully conscious. His light humor and his keen satire of the Sofia of his day were something new in Bulgarian literature, a further development of the old Bay-Ganyu, and he was really the founder and the most distinguished exponent of Bulgarian comedy of character.

There were many other authors of this period both in prose and verse who rose above the level of mediocrity. The majority of them were relatively simple men, well educated, well aware of the nature of the Bulgarian people, who illustrated in their works the national character and the Bulgarian landscape. Such were Ivan Rakitin (1885-1934), Damyan Kalfov, a prose writer and a writer of comedies (b. 1887) and Racho Stoyanov whose drama, *The Masters,* had a great success. Still another was Stiliyan Chilingirov (b. 1881) whose poetry won him considerable fame and who developed still further the Bulgarian-Ukrainian literary relations.

There were several excellent critics such as Iordan Badev, who was attached to the National Theatre and wrote extensively for some of the best critical reviews in Bulgaria. He remained free from all the *clichés* of the various literary groups, and in the *Sketches of the Living* he spoke his mind freely and openly about his contemporaries. So too did Anna Kameneva (b. 1894), the daughter of a prominent Bulgarian diplomat.

She had many opportunities to travel, and she made herself the exponent of British and American literary criticism and applied it to Bulgarian literature. Around her clustered all of those Bulgarians who were interested in Anglo-American civilization and culture.

Another writer who can be mentioned is K. Petkanov (b. 1891), who published many stories on the Bulgarian countryside and who knew the peasants and their life very well, especially those in the region of Thrace. He took a prominent part in the agitation for the return to Bulgaria of this area where he was born. While he was not a first-rate writer, he was not without considerable ability.

Another member of the younger generation was Angel Karaliychev (b. 1902), who early became a member of the *Zlatorog* group. His vague and yet definite stories have much in common with expressionism, and in his use of legends both in stories for children and for adults he approached the manner of Todorov and the latter's way of retelling folktales in a modern form. Then there were other writers such as Vladimir Polyanov and poets such as Iordan Strubel who were just approaching maturity and had not yet found themselves when the storm of World War II broke over Europe.

By early 1939 popular interest had come to center on the historical school of writing. There were long historical novels such as *The Angel-Voiced Singer* of Dobri Nemirov and many other well-known names. There were popular accounts of Bulgarian history from the earliest times and there were even weekly pamphlets, the *Bulgarian Historical Library,* in which writers of all grades of excellence published little sixteen-page stories, in a small format, on some phase of Bulgarian history. These histories in fictional form were written to express the sorrow of the Bulgarian people at their failure to hold and retain those parts of the Bulgarian ethnographic territory which they had had during the First and Second Bulgarian Empires and had won in the First Balkan War. In the feverish atmosphere of 1938 and 1939, all of these propaganda stories (sometimes well-written and sometimes very crude) served to arouse popular sentiment, especially among the students, against all of their neighbors without exception, especially Romania because of her occupation of the Dobrudja. These little histories helped pave the way for Bulgaria's new alliance with Nazi Germany and Fascist Italy, the preliminary for the downfall of the regime and the ending of the period that had commenced with Father Paisi and expanded after the liberation in 1876.

CHAPTER ELEVEN

Toward Communism

In the preceding chapter we have traced the course of Bulgarian literature between the two World Wars. The national mood was one of humiliation and later of defiance. The writers were largely under the influence of Symbolism and Modernism, under the leadership of men who had been trained in the West, if they had been abroad. The Russian influence came largely from the Russian classics and the Russian Symbolists. The old tradition of drawing subjects from peasant life still remained strong, even though the leading authors had adopted many of the modern methods of working and the newer techniques. There was, however, a latent strain of influence exerted by the Russian Revolution.

Marxist philosophy made its appearance in Bulgaria in the eighteen nineties largely through the influence of Dimitar Blagoyev (1855-1924) who had studied in Russia under the early Russian Marxists. He found the Bulgarians very inhospitable to Marxism, because there was but a small urban proletariat at the time. As in Russia the early Marxists had no message for the peasant population who were desirous of bettering their own conditions and of securing more land for their family use. There were after the liberation from the Turks no large latifundia. The peasants wanted better educational and agricultural facilities for their own land, and the purely doctrinaire teachings of the Marxists with their hostility to God and private property left them relatively unmoved.

Here and there Blagoyev found a few converts but those converts, when they achieved prominence, much preferred to ally themselves with the prevailing trend of peasant Populism which inveighed against the usurers, the rich urban families and the upper bourgeoisie, whom in their hearts they secretly envied. This was why the criticism of Aleko Konstantinov and his friends who made fun of the pretensions of the lesser officials and the crudities of society bore such rich fruits and dominated Bulgarian thought until the Balkan Wars. Even most of Blagoyev's admirers adopted a loose definition of socialism that displeased his stricter followers. It is safe to say that if the disturbances in the Balkans had ceased with the triumph of Bulgaria and her allies over the decaying Ottoman Empire, the future of the country would have been very different and the democratic traditions of the Bulgarians would have borne rich fruit.

The disasters suffered by Bulgaria in the Second Balkan War and World War I completely changed the picture. Popular discontent knew no bounds, and, after the abdication of Tsar Ferdinand, his son Tsar Boris III had difficulty in asserting his authority. In the meanwhile the Russian Communist Revolution had taken place. Lenin was in the saddle, and the spectacle of a socialistic-communistic regime governing that great neighbor which had so often helped Bulgaria could not fail to have its effect.

When Stamboliyski took power in September, 1918, the peasants seemed fully to come into their own. They were wearied by the three wars which had exhausted the country and had shattered all of Bulgaria's hopes. They welcomed their leader's attempt to make peace with their neighbors, even though it meant the sacrifice of their national ambitions, especially in Macedonia. They also hoped that certain concessions to Bulgaria incorporated in the Treaty of Neuilly would be carried into effect by the victorious powers. Again, for a moment, there seemed hopes for a peaceful settlement.

Stamboliyski's policy, however, united against him all classes of the population. His measures not only alienated the rich and the military classes but many of the intelligentsia, and, as time passed, they all combined in a single opposition. To add to his difficulties, a violent movement developed among the Macedonians demanding incorporation with Bulgaria. When Stamboliyski did not countenance this, they too joined the opposition.

Communist agitators came into the country from Russia, and toward them he adopted an ambiguous policy. On the one hand he used them against the bourgeoisie in the cities and supported measures similar to those adopted by the Bolsheviks in Russia. On the other hand he checked their activity among the peasants, thus arousing their dislikes as he had that of all classes except the hard-working Bulgarian peasants.

The opposition to Stamboliyski finally took definite form and a sudden uprising of the military and their supporters on June 8 and 9, 1923 overthrew the government. Stamboliyski was killed and a reactionary government commenced to rule with great brutality but it did not dare to touch his agrarian reforms which remained in effect until World War II. It was followed by disturbances amounting almost to civil war. Then as peace seemed to be coming back, the Communists made an attempt to murder Tsar Boris by planting a bomb in the Cathedral in Sofia.

This peasant uprising, followed by a distinctively Communist movement, furnished the background for those writers who are now claimed, with some basis of truth, by the Communists as examples of the socially "progressive" Bulgarian literature. These writers were then young men who had been fascinated by the Communist experiment in Russia and were trying to bring about something of the same sort in Bulgaria under very different conditions. Their lives and fate were markedly similar, and, behind the Communist praises, we can see the doubts that came into the minds of these writers as to whether they were correct in their judgments.

The dean of this group was Dimitar I. Polyanov, who was the first Bulgarian author to present socialistic themes in literature and was, in fact, the teacher of many of the younger men of this group. He commenced to write in 1895 under the influence of Blagoyev. For fifty years he continued his activity, and his work was commemorated in 1945. Yet, Communist critics do not hesitate to say that even he did not appreciate the full meaning of the Marxist-Leninist teaching, because "he repeated esoteric symbolistic phrases which undermined the class struggle. He speaks of the future in general words, 'the dawn of a free life,' 'the rise of a bright day,' etc."[1] Polyanov was aiming at a free society, an ideal existence, and not the dictatorship of the proletariat, which was demanded by the course of events.

His pupil, Khristo Smirnensky (1898-1923), who died in the attempted revolution of 1923, was more satisfactory. He started his life as a symbolist, "but he quickly saw that war is a misfortune for the people, although he still did rtot understand the social causes of war."[2] It was only under the example of Soviet successes that he really came to appreciate the truth, and then it was too late. Khristo Yasenkov (1889-1925) and N. Rumyantsev (1896-1925) also made mistakes in their careers, but these were natural to the leaders of the Peasant Union, which preached "the full independence of the peasant movement."

Geo Milev, or Georgi Kasabov (1895-1925), is a more interesting example. It is true that he saw the revolt of 1923 "not as an organized struggle of the workers and peasants, guided by the Communist Party, but as an elemental revolt of a mass aroused to anger." At the same time the Communists admit that in his work in the National Theatre he did his best to turn the course of the Bulgarian stage into what were, to them, socially productive channels.

This movement, later adopted by Communism, had a strong agrarian and idealistic tinge and was in essence a revolt against the extremely artificial methods of the modernists and some of their Nietzschean views. It was inspired by the national sorrow over Bulgaria's defeats, and if the majority of these men had not died at the hands of the reactionary parties, they would not have received that aureole of martyrdom which has insured their survival in Communist Bulgaria. During the period before World War II, their memory was treasured by small underground circles but they found little response among the great mass of the reading public.

A somewhat different case is offered by Lyudmil Stoyanov who was born in 1888 and educated partly in Sofia and partly in Lviv. Stoyanov has been a prolific writer since 1916 in both prose and verse and has passed through a number of stages in his long career. He was at first heavily influenced by Symbolism and indeed for a while, along with Trayanov, was the editor of *Hyperion,* but his works always had a leftist orientation. With the rise of Nazism and Fascism, he swung very decidedly to the left and finally about 1930 more or less definitely allied himself with Communism. Still, for several years he did not burn his bridges behind him and continued to work in his own vein. In fact, in 1934 he published a novel, *Stamboliyski the Agrarian Apostle,* in which he warmly defended the agrarian point of view. It is small wonder that some of the literary critics of the early thirties found themselves wondering what was the real faith of Stoyanov who was publishing his works in journals of quite different political camps and adjusting his ideas to the medium where he was going to publish. Yet, since the introduction of Communism into the country, he has become the President of the Union of Bulgarian Writers. Now in his old age he has the honor of being considered the dean of the Bulgarian Communist authors and their most outstanding representative among the older men.

Another author who may be placed here is Stoyan Zagorchinov. He is typical of some of the lesser writers of the day. Although he commenced to publish before 1912, his first important work was the *Legends of St. Sofia* (1926), a description of the clashes between the Bulgarians and the Byzantines in the sixth century. The story attracted little attention. It is to be classed rather with those imbued by mysticism and religion, but it did show the author's absorption in history and prepared the way for his later work. His masterpiece, *The Last Day,* began to appear in 1931 after he had worked on it for several years, and it has been republished by the Communists. It gives a picture of the social clashes between the Tsar and the boyars in the last days of the Second Bulgarian Empire before the Turkish conquest. The real hero is the semi-mythical *hayduk,* Momchil, who by popular tradition was connected with the family of King Marko. Though a simple *hayduk,* he was in love with a princess. The story involves the efforts of the Bulgarians to secure freedom from the oppressions of the nobles. While the author is not always historically accurate, as in the influence which he ascribes to the Bogomils at that period (a favorite theme of the day), he mercilessly chastizes the upper classes. In 1943, during the

war, he published the *Hand of Ilya,* a drama on a historical subject again much in the manner of his first works. In 1950 he
reworked it into a novel, *The Festival in Boyana.* In all of these
works Zagorchinov showed himself responsive to those chords
which have been fully exploited by the Communists.

The same is true of Svetoslav Minkov, who in these years bitterly caricatured the capitalistic world, especially America. His
works, relatively unimportant when they first appeared, were
later republished, and Minkov has been declared a successful
exponent of critical realism on its way to socialist realism.

Another writer of the same type was Khristyu Belev, whose
fiftieth birthday has recently been commemorated. By 1932 he
was associated with Georgi Dimitrov, the Bulgarian Communist
leader. In 1936 he published his novel, *The Break,* a work
which he had written during one of his prison sentences for
Communist activity in the Balkans. He fought in Spain in the
International Brigade and in 1937 visited the Soviet Union
and wrote a book on his experiences. Since the coming of the
Communists to power, he has become a popular and official
writer.

Thus between the two wars, Bulgarian Communism had
sunk no real roots in the population. It was usually a feeble
offshoot from the Agrarian stem and had at its disposal only
minor authors who attracted little attention from the peasant
masses or the bulk of the intellectuals. It won a hearing only
because Russia, the big brother of Bulgaria, was under Communist rule and many Bulgarians continued to want connections with that Slavic country which had helped them in 1876
and on other occasions. To win that connection, there were
many who were willing to close their eyes to what was happening
in the Soviet Union and to view Communism as a typically Russian problem exactly as the older men who were fighting for a
free Bulgaria did not raise questions about what Russia was
doing at home, so long as the tsars would give help to the Bulgarians. This was cleverly realized by the Communists as was
shown in 1939 when Molotov visited Sofia in connection with
the showing of the Soviet film, *Alexander Nevsky,* and devoted

a great deal of attention to the monuments to Russia in Bulgaria. Not the least of these was the Cathedral of St. Alexander, erected after the liberation in memory of the Tsar-Liberator, Alexander II, who had done so much for the final liberation of Bulgaria in those fateful years after 1876.

CHAPTER TWELVE

The Communist Period

World War II, which began in September, 1939, opened another tragic period in Bulgarian history and literature. The nation, embittered by the defeats of the past and aroused by the nationalistic successes of Nazi Germany and Fascist Italy, was only too ready to embark on new adventures that promised to accomplish the long postponed satisfaction of the Bulgarian desires to unify the Bulgarian ethnographic territory and to bring under Bulgarian control those lands which had once belonged to the First Bulgarian Empire.

In the years preceding 1939 there had come a slight official tolerance of the Soviet regime as a form of the traditional Russophile sentiments that were held in certain quarters. The first Soviet play, Katayev's *A Thousand Troubles,* was produced in 1935. Then came Shvarkin's *A Strange Child* in 1936 and, during the period of Nazi-Soviet friendship, *Platon Krechet* by the Soviet Ukrainian author, Alexander Korniychuk. All met with success.

To some extent Nazi influence grew in Bulgaria. The celebration of the fiftieth anniversary of the foundation of the University of Sofia (renamed the University of St. Clement of Okhrida) was dominated by the Nazis who behaved in the most ludicrous fashion possible. Yet, at the same time no one in Sofia doubted that there was going to be a Nazi-Soviet alliance against the democratic powers, and this gave a considerable free hand to the sympathizers with Communism, until the German attack upon the Soviet Union in 1941.

To draw Bulgaria still further into the Nazi net, Germany transferred from Romania to Bulgaria the rule over the Dobrudja, a Bulgarian territory, and after the Nazi-Fascist invasion of Greece and Yugoslavia, allowed the Bulgarians to take possession of territory that they desired from those lands. When the storm broke in 1941, Bulgaria declared war on the Western powers but not on the Soviet Union. This at the time was more symbolic than real, for the events of 1941 bade fair to separate the country even more decidedly from any contact with the Soviets, and there were not lacking those who realized that a Bulgarian-Soviet friendship would bring up again that danger of Russian colonialism which Tsar Alexander II had tried to impose upon Bulgaria after 1877.

Tsar Boris died mysteriously on August 28, 1943. The Nazi tide was already ebbing. The regency for the young Tsar Simeon, headed by the Tsar's brother, Prince Kiril, and Prof. Bogdan Filov, a great archeologist but an unsuccessful and weak statesman, tried to extricate Bulgaria from the Nazi clutches as the Soviet armies approached the Bulgarian borders. They broke with Germany, approached the Western allies, set up a liberal government and then declared war upon Germany. It proved of no avail, for the Soviet armies continued to invade Bulgaria and seized and executed the members of the regency and their chief supporters. The Western allies, still desirous of maintaining a unified front with the Soviet Union, did little more than register formal protests and accepted Stalin's arguments for his treatment of the Bulgarians. When the smoke cleared away, the so-called Fatherland Front that replaced the liberal government, contrary to the Soviet promises to its allies, proved to be a unitary Communist government under the control of Georgi M. Dimitrov, an old Bulgarian Communist who had been "involved" in Germany in the Reichstag fire after the accession of Hitler. This government consistently attacked the United States. When it proceeded to execute some of the Bulgarian leaders on the ground that they were American agents, the United States broke with the new Bulgarian regime, and Bulgaria remained behind the iron curtain, almost as completely sealed off from the free world as Albania.

The Communists at once set to work to remodel the entire country on the Russian Soviet pattern. They introduced collective farms, commenced a process of rapid enforced industrialization and declared hostile every one and every institution in all fields that questioned the superiority of Russian Communist culture. Henceforth there was to be no one in Bulgaria who dared to think on any pattern that was not approved in Moscow.

In this atmosphere literature was supposed to be cut to those patterns of Socialist Realism that had been approved by Stalin and Zhdanov. Free thought and writing became impossible. Nearly all of the older and better known authors, who had maintained their independence even during the most disturbed periods of the last decades, relapsed into silence if they were not physically removed from the scene, and only a few authors, like Lyudmil Stoyanov, put themselves willingly at the disposal of the new regime. Henceforth Bulgarian literature was to be the work of the few men who had tried to write against the regime of Tsar Boris and the new men whom they intended to train themselves.

The Communists, not satisfied with this, then set themselves to rewrite the history of the past. Their easiest task was to fit Botev into the new scheme of history. He had always been thoroughly in tune with the Russian radicals as well as the radicals of western Europe, but it may be doubted whether Botev, in his wildest moments, would have been satisfied with the stifling despotism that was foisted upon the Bulgarian people in the name of a People's Democracy. Vazov was more difficult to incorporate into the new version of history, for only his early works from the time of the liberation, when he welcomed the Russian armed forces in Bulgaria, met Communist standards. The greatest praise was awarded to those men such as Rakovski, who had died before the liberation and who, consequently, had taken no part in the complex process of setting up and making function a Bulgarian monarchical state. They had kind words for the supporters of Stamboliyski and the Agrarians, but they never allowed their readers to forget that these men were in their own way idealists who understood little or nothing of Marxism, even though they had fought and died bravely in the defence of the rights of the peasants and the proletariat. They treated them as the Russians had treated the Ukrainian *Borotbisty* who in the nineteen twenties were flattered, used by the Communists, and then liquidated when their usefulness was at an end.

Naturally the translation of the works of Soviet Russian literature was carried on with ever increasing speed. It was done not only to give the Bulgarians true patterns of Communist literature but also to provide occasions for stressing Russian accomplishments and the willing assistance of the older brother in these critical times. In the period from 1945 to 1950 more than forty Soviet plays were produced on the Bulgarian stage and all independent officials or actors like Trifon Kunev, a former symbolist poet who was Director of the National Theatre, were accused of being part of the American spy ring and were at best removed from their posts.

Under such models and the instructions to follow the patterns set by Gorky, Sholokhov and the other Soviet greats, the Communists finally developed a new set of writers, who were willing to produce works that were Soviet and socialist in essence and Bulgarian only in setting. Such were the poets Anton Rastsvetnikov, who had begun to write before World War II and was just winning recognition, and Krum Kyulyakov (b. 1893). They drew the inspiration for their work (poems, plays, and stories) from the troubled times before 1944 and the underground activity of the partisans opposing the Nazis. Some of the new works by such men as A. Gulyashki were praised, but almost invariably the critics, under Soviet inspiration and following the example set by Moscow, pointed out the flaws and defects in them. They were either too personal, too absorbed in the problems of the individual, or they failed to indicate the strength of the popular acceptance of the Communists as sole leaders and sole guides to the promised land of socialism. There is hardly a single volume by any of the younger men or women which has been accepted wholeheartedly as giving a fitting description of Bulgarian reality in the terms of the required Socialist Realism.

Perhaps the play by Lozan Strelkov, *The Reconnaissance,* the story of the unmasking of a mysterious woman spy, was given the most praise for solving the problem without being theatrical or sensational and for presenting the facts truly. Orlin Vasilev pub-

lished a successful novel, *A Hayduk Does Not Feed His Mother,*
and various stories on the underground, while the poet Kamen
Zidarov in 1948 in a play called *The Tsar's Mercy* castigated the
treachery of Tsar Ferdinand who only grants to a poor widow
who has once saved his life the mercy of having the body of her
revolutionary son returned to her instead of it being buried
in a nameless grave.

All these and many other works from the early years found
their main themes in the events of World War I, the following
disturbances and the partisan activity during World War II.
A break was made in 1949 when the theme of social reconstruc-
tion emerged into the foreground in the play, *The Promise,*
by Andrey Gulyashki. This play was typical of one stage of
Soviet literature, when the object was to present the hero encouraging the men in a factory to fulfill their norm of production
despite all difficulties, personal conflicts in his own family,
the activity of wreckers inspired from abroad, and material difficulties caused by the setting of the norm at too high a level,
while the workers respond with their Communist sense of responsibility, and all ends well with the opponents and saboteurs
happily punished.

It would be boring and needless to go into the details of the
individual works of these years. They follow a traditional and
stereotyped pattern for the various themes and can be differentiated only by the quality of the language and the style. It is in
the full sense a standardized and regimented literature, and
even then it barely received the approval of the Central Committee of the Bulgarian Communist Party which scrutinized
minutely the smallest details to see that they corresponded accu-
rately to the general line of the Party at the moment when the
work came up for discussion.

Meanwhile the Bulgarian reading public was flooded with
Russian books and with Bulgarian translations of Russian
books. Official visits of Bulgarians to the land of the "older
brother," Moscow, and of Russian writers to Bulgaria went on
at a great rate. Everything was done to strengthen the Russian
influence on all fields of Bulgarian life. The keynote to this was
set by Dimitrov in 1947, when he said:

"There is not and cannot be a right thinking person who would not be convinced that true friendship with the Soviet Union is as necessary for the national independence and flowering of Bulgaria as the sun and air are for every living creature."

Vulko Chervenkov, the successor of Dimitrov after the latter's illness and death, added in 1949:

"The unbreakable Bulgarian-Soviet friendship is the main basis for our existence as an independent nation. Without the unbreakable Bulgarian-Soviet friendship, without our sincere gratitude and loyalty to the Soviet Union, the tested and wise VKP (b), and Comrade Stalin, the national independence of our country would have been unthinkable. There can be no real Bulgarian patriotism without these feelings."

On this basis the entire Bulgarian literary life and culture were transformed. All writers who hoped for publication were compelled to join the Society of Bulgarian Writers formed on the Russian Soviet pattern. Its first president was Lyudmil Stoyanov. Many of the former successful writers were conspicuous by their failure to join or were refused permission to enter the new group and continue their work. All the old literary journals were abolished and replaced by new ones. Among these latter were the *Literary Front, September,* and in 1957, *The Flame* (Plamuk). All of them were closely supervised by the Society of Bulgarian Writers and by the appropriate Ministries of the government and the Central Committee of the Party, which was only too glad to point out ideological defects in the works of any of the writers.

After the death of Stalin, there came a slight change in the situation, although the old tradition of Russian friendship kept the writers in Bulgaria from going so far and so fast as they did in Poland and Hungary. Yet there were signs that the same process of revolt against the narrow form of Socialist Realism was taking place. Some of the younger writers, especially after Khrushchev's denunciation of Stalin at the Twentieth Congress of the Communist Party in February, 1956, expressed themselves in terms that were highly reminiscent of the Russian novel of Dudintsev, *Not by Bread Alone.* The tendency increased still more strongly after the demotion of Vulko Chervenkov in April, 1956. Writers, even those trained under Communism, began to point out the psychological failings inherent in mankind and to indicate that not all Communists had reached that state of perfection and selfless devotion that socialist realism called for and presumed to exist. They became in a way pessimistic and ceased to picture only the improvement of conditions under the benign rule of the Party.

Thus Emil Manov published a novel, *The Unauthentic Case.* In this tale the hero (?) is a good, sincere Communist, but after his marriage and a certain rise in the Party ranks, he returns to an old love, finally starts to drink, and in the end goes insane. Manov was criticized because he did not represent the other Party members in the novel as exercising enough kindly and fatherly supervision over the hero to return him to his sense of obligation to his family and the Party but allowed him to proceed on his way to self-destruction.

Todor Genov, another Communist, in a play named *Fear,* made his hero a former partisan and a man possessed of almost all vices and, yet, one who was able to control himself and as a careerist rise in the Party hierarchy and even aspire to the post of a Minister. He even included a parody on a poem by one of the conformist writers, Khristo Radevski, *To the Party,* in these words:

"Lead me, Party, lead me, I am ready to sacrifice all.
Send me abroad if you wish, even there I will answer
your call,
I am your son, and if you wish you may make me
a Minister,
With flowers I will adorn every home, happy days
will flow,
Only give me an office and a throne and I will repay you
an hundredfold."

Since Genov did not make it clear that such individuals were removed from even the highest posts by the watchdogs of the

Party, he was directly satirizing and slandering the Party as a whole.

The poet Krum Penev was accused of writing and submitting to various publications such anti-Communist verse that it scandalized even the non-Communist members of the staff.

P. Neznakomov in *The Flame* published the story, *The Benefactors*, which described the same forms of oppression of the poor by the rich that occurred in the old capitalistic society and still existed under Communist rule.

Kiril Toromanski in the *Literary Front*, the official writers' paper, in a short story, *Anna the Comrade of the District*, shows how an earnest worker was persecuted by a tyrannical chief, who cared little for the population of his district and scorned them at every turn. To add to the insult, the story appeared in the same number of the journal which contained a scathing indictment of all those writers who did not treat the Party as sacrosanct.

Even Lyudmil Stoyanov ventured in some of his articles to assert that artistic truth did not always agree with the general line of the Party and that the author should be free to follow that artistic truth to some degree, even if it did contradict the general line. It was a very mild plea for the independence of the writer, but it was at any rate a straw in the wind.

The writers were further accused of circulating illegally manuscript copies of works which could not hope to pass the official requirements, lax as they had become. In a word, there was every indication that part at least of the Bulgarian writers, poets and dramatists, and even critics like Gocho Gochev, the editor of the periodical *Theatre*, and Mikhail Velichkov were infected with a dangerous spirit of opposition to the directives of the Party. After the demotion of Chervenkov they even ventured to demand a special Party Congress to implement still further the decrees of the Twentieth Congress against the cult of personality.

There were of course writers like Lozan Strelkov, Khristo Radevski, and Kamen Kalchev who stoutly defended the Party line and denounced this trend to revisionism as the result of Western bourgeois machinations. They obeyed fully all the orders of the Central Committee and cheerfully argued for the official positions and for the fact that any deviation from the principles of Socialist Realism was treason to Marxism-Leninism. The extent to which they were willing to go was shown by Radevski in his poem *To the Party:*

"And if I should ever forget myself
And start to slander you—
Don't spit at me!— For then
Such honor I would not deserve,
Not even the honor of your spittle!"

On August 29, 1957 Khrushchev declared in Moscow the necessity for the control of literature by the Party, reasserting the general principles which had been enforced by Stalin and Zhdanov. This speech did not pass unnoticed in Bulgaria. From November 29 to December 1, 1957 there was held in Sofia a meeting of the party organization of the Society of Bulgarian Writers attended by Riben Avramov, the member of the Central Committee in charge of science, culture and education, and Dimitar Ganev, a Secretary of the Central Committee and a member of the Politburo, to silence the disputants. The secretary, A. Gulyashki, made a formal report listing ten writers who had first come into prominence under the Communist regime. With the exception of Stoyanov, who had long been regarded as the most devoted servant of the Party, the men who had been infected, as in Poland and Hungary, were Communist-trained, Communist-educated and so could not have known personally the bitter struggles that went on in 1923 or during World War II. The writers like Zidarov, Manov, Genov, and others made perfunctory apologies for some of their misdeeds, but their excuses were so obviously hypocritical, or even sarcastic, that it was obvious no mere resolution was going to bring them back to the conventional path.

In April the Society of Bulgarian Writers held its annual meeting, at which Todor Zhivkov, the First Secretary of the Central Committee of the Party, appeared to condemn the malcontents and to stress the fact that the "concept of spontaneous development of literature and art is alien to our Party, our Marxism-Leninism." At the same time he appealed to the writers in the hope that unity could be restored without the use of those forcible measures which were so freely employed during the regime of Stalin.

It is already obvious that the Communists prefer to see this oppositional trend as directly inspired by western counter-revolutionary influences. They do not hesitate to accuse the West of corrupting the writers. At the same time they have prepared their own diagnosis of the ills from which the writers are suffering. These include traditionalism and, on the other hand, pseudo-innovationism (to be sought in the attempts to acclimate the forms used by Hemingway and Camus). There is epigonism, the attempt to write in the tradition of the past writers and to present more or less closely the old Bulgarian village, as an escape from the attempts to picture the turmoil of collectivization. There are also *chernogledstvo*—a pessimistic outlook on modern life—and empiricism and descriptionalism—terms used to describe life without fulfilling those demands set by Socialist Realism.

Still more basic was the dispute as to the way in which socialist romanticism could be treated in its relation to Socialist Realism. Should this be included? Or separated? It was duly declared that any separation of the romantic and the realistic was anti-Marxian. In still another dispute, in order to remove the temptation to hark back to the older periods, it was declared that the critical realism of the past had nothing in common with the Socialist Realism of the present:

"To-day's society and to-day's State have nothing in common with the social conditions and institutions of the past, for our contemporary social order is based precisely on those virtues which our predecessors extolled while that which they rejected has either ceased to exist, or exists as something discarded and condemned to extinction. In these circumstances our realism can only be a positive one. It says 'Yes' to our socialist reality. That is why it is called Socialist Realism."

Here the situation apparently stands at present. The staffs of the various periodicals have been thoroughly purged, but apparently no violence or arrests have resulted. The next step will apparently rest upon the Bulgarian writers, some of whom have manifestly yielded to the pressure, and still more upon the will of the Kremlin and its decision on how to handle the situation. Khrushchev late in the spring visited the Communist Party Congress in Sofia to inveigh against Tito and revisionism in general, but there seems in the different countries, including the USSR, a disinclination to resort to force at this time. The future cannot, of course, be predicted.

A special feature in the Russian attempt to eliminate any discontent is rather curious. As we have seen, the early Bulgarian writers were much influenced by the Ukrainian revival, which had a strong anti-Russian tinge. Now that the Kremlin has produced, more or less to its satisfaction, a Soviet Ukrainian literature which is subservient to Russian influences and hints, it has fostered very lively Bulgarian-Ukrainian relations, a continued exchange of Ukrainian-Bulgarian Communist writers and a systematic publication in the two lands of articles expressing the Communist character of the other. Thus after stifling Ukrainian thought, Russian Communism is trying to use its resulting product to inspire in Bulgaria a general sense of a Russian-led Slavic Communist union, apparently to offset any tendency in Bulgaria to sympathize with Tito, Yugoslavia, or their revisionist brand of Communism.

Thus by 1958 Bulgarian literature at home has been standardized as completely as possible on the Russian Communist model. Some of the efforts seem to be unpalatable, thanks to the Bulgarian spirit of independence which has not been crushed, as it was not in the past, by the existence of pro-Russian sentiments. The Bulgarian Communist writers resent the utterly unpersonalized literature and the dogmatic *clichés* imposed upon them. Whether the Communists can master this resentment is the question of the future.

The Characteristics of Bulgarian Literature

It is almost two centuries since Father Paisi Khilandarski, a humble and obscure monk on Mount Athos, conceived the idea of compiling a history of the Bulgarians as an ideal toward which his oppressed people could work in the future. The response to his work was painfully slow, but gradually and surely his book extended its influence, first among the clergy and the monks, and then among the educated laymen in the Bulgarian colonies in the Russian Empire and especially in such Ukrainian cities as Odesa and Nizhyn, and also at home. These Bulgarians were inspired not only by the Russians with whom they were in contact but perhaps still more by the Ukrainians, who in a similar situation were becoming painfully aware of their own national individuality. The Bulgarians were entranced by the works of Kvitka-Osnovyanenko and especially by the great Ukrainian poet and political martyr, Taras Shevchenko, with his strong pleas for nationalism, democracy, and social justice.

Within a century men like Petko Slaveykov were writing real poetry, were evaluating the old Bulgarian peasant culture, and were turning the folksongs and traditions of their people to good use. They struggled first for a Bulgarian national Church and school and secured both. Others worked to produce a Bulgarian press. They did it. Still others in the *hayduk* tradition fought with arms in their hands against their oppressors.

By the time of Karavelov and Botev the movement had engulfed almost the entire population. The Turkish massacres of 1876 focussed the attention of Europe and especially of Russia upon the Bulgarians. The Russians offered them help as brother Slavs, but the Bulgarian leaders after liberation soon showed that they had no intention of becoming the permanent vassals of Russia. They wanted to play their own role and they did.

The literary movement went on. Vazov pitched its note on a world-wide scale and was the first Bulgarian author to have a novel translated into all the European languages. The men of his generation gradually developed a literary taste, and while they did not form a distinct school, they were bound together by their ideals.

From here it was but a short step for the generation that matured in the nineties to look further. The leading men, trained in Germany and influenced by Mykhaylo Drahomaniv, a Ukrainian who became a professor in Sofia, introduced into Bulgarian literature in a Bulgarian form all those literary movements which were developing in Europe, and they proved themselves worthy disciples. They used these new styles to express themselves and the ideals of their people, to integrate Bulgarian literature with that of the whole of Europe, and to translate the leading European classics into Bulgarian.

At the moment of Bulgaria's highest hopes, there came the Balkan Wars and then World War I. The lights went out all over Europe, and they have not yet been relighted. There came the Russian Revolution with the efforts of the non-Russian peoples to escape from the rule of Moscow and the triumph of Russian Communism. Bulgaria had to pass through terrible times. The new generation which held the centre of the stage in the nineteen twenties could not escape the depressing atmosphere which hung over the country. Yet, after years of mysticism and doubt, the country emerged into a prosperity and an order which it had not known for centuries and which the literature reflected.

Hope revived but in a form that led Bulgaria to enter World War II on the side of the Fascist and Nazi powers. The result was a new catastrophe, for when the Nazis were expelled, the Red Army proceeded with typical cynicism and ruthlessness to set up a Communist government in Bulgaria and to root out all typically Bulgarian traditions and turn the state into a

Communist satellite where no one could breathe freely and everything was on the Muscovite pattern. Bulgarian literature, by fair means and foul, was degraded to be merely a subordinate part of Russian Soviet literature. The Russian Communist dictatorship is a tyranny worse than that of the Turks, for they only oppressed the body and did not try to crush the soul of the Bulgarian people. That soul is not yet dead, for even the most slavish Communists at the slightest opportunity have tried to express their own thoughts and feelings.

What are the chief characteristics of this new Bulgarian literature? The answer is relatively simple.

(1) It is for the most part in its origin and development a peasant literature, deeply rooted in the Bulgarian folklore. It is the literature of a proud and independent peasantry, tillers of the soil, who educated and trained themselves to the point where they won their independence against overwhelming odds. The decade when they won it, the seventies of the last century, was the heroic period of modern Bulgarian history.

(2) It is this period when independence was won which supplied many of the main themes even down to World War II and which in various modes of treatment and various *genres* formed the subject matter of many of the greatest works.

As a corollary to this we have the fact that Sofia, although the capital and the educational centre of the country, has never been a city that elicited the literary sympathies of the writers. In recent years they have lived and written in its neighborhood, but it is Tirnovo, the capital of the Second Bulgarian Empire, that has figured more heavily in poems and in prose. So, too, have the little villages scattered throughout the land, for it is these and their customs that have been the models for the authors.

(3) A special feature of Bulgarian literature is its strong sense of the past. The great days of Bulgaria were those of the First and Second Empires and they have exerted a disproportionate influence on the thinking of the Bulgarian nation. This has favored the development of the historical novel and historical poetry sometimes at the cost of injury to their historical perspective.

(4) Throughout the entire period the call for a democratic

world outlook and for the understanding and preservation of human rights has been a dominant feature in all of the major writers. It has encouraged the Bulgarian love of liberty and freedom and has given a sober and realistic tone to the entire literature even in the twentieth century when the Bulgarians were for the first time becoming conscious of life outside of their native villages.

(5) The present of Bulgarian literature is dark and so will its future be until the yoke of Communism is broken and the Bulgarians are once more free to choose their own path into the future and develop their own traditions and institutions. But that time will surely come.

The Bulgarians have travelled far over a hard road during the past two centuries. They have done well and they deserve the sympathy and assistance of the free world. The burden of the past has been borne by the Bulgarian peasant, thrifty, hard-working, patient and suffering. The literature deals with his hopes, his troubles and his difficulties. It is a good basis for a literature that is both idealistic and realistic and we can be sure that a liberated Bulgaria will take its place in the free world of the future and resume its interrupted course of development.

Selections of Bulgarian Poetry

Bulgarian Folksongs

THE SLAVE GANGS

O thou hill, thou high green hill!
Why, green hill, art thou so withered?
Why so withered and so wilted?
Did the winter's frost so wilt thee?
Did the summer's heat so parch thee?
Not the winter's frost did wilt me,
Nor the summer's heat did parch me,
But my glowing heart is smothered.
Yesterday three slave gangs crossed me;
Grecian maids were in the first row,
Weeping, crying bitterly:
"O our wealth! art lost for ever!"
Black eyed maidens from Walachia
Weeping, crying in the second:
"O ye ducats of Walachia!"
Bulgar women in the third row,
Weeping, crying, "O sweet home!
O sweet home! beloved children!
Fare ye well, fare well for ever!

J. S. C. de Radius, *Russian and Slavic Poetry*
London, 1854, pp. 56-57.

II

If it's flowers that you want,
Then, O youth, come in the morning,
'Tis the time when happy flowers
Will reciprocate your love.

167

If it's water that you want,
Then, I pray you, come at noon,
'Tis the time when laughing water
Will reciprocate your love.

If it's love that you desire,
Then, O youth, come in the twilight,
And perhaps a lovely maiden
Will reciprocate your love.

The Shade of the Balkans, p. 121.

III

Neda, lovely Neda
Lay on the bed of sickness.
When they sowed the fields
Illness came upon her.
When they reaped the fields
Illness had not flown.
Then said she to her mother:
Lift me up in your arms,
Take me to the courtyard
That I may have sight of the sun,
That he may have sight of me.
And as they were on the threshold,
The friends of Neda came past,
They came to work in the fields.
They sang and it was for her:

Rise, Neda, and come with us,
Make an end of your sickness,
Come and finish the work
That you began in the spring.

Neda lifted her eyes,
She moved her lips in reply,
She sank on the ground and was dead.

The Shade of the Balkans, pp. 126-127.

IV

THE DEATH OF MARKO

There in the castle, at the lofty battlement,
With his friend of friends sat the King's son Marko,
With his friend of friends, Philip the Hungarian,
And the wife of Marko, the fair young wife, attended them,
Filling their cups with the noble wine.
Then it was they gazed o'er the plain of Prilip
And unto Marko spoke Philip the Hungarian:
Knowest thou what has befallen the world?
Never dost thou sally forth beyond the threshold,
As if the world had naught save the beauty of thy wife;
And what befalls—of that thou knowest nothing.
There is invented a death-bringing engine,
And inside it there dwells a little ball,
Out it flies and strikes a man—out flies the soul of him.
Then laughed Marko at the words of Philip,
Marko laughed and his wife was smiling,
And these were the words of the old, great-hearted hero:
Widely, forsooth, my friend, hast thou travelled,
Too well thou knowest what happens in the world,
How can a ball kill a gallant hero?
Philip the Hungarian raised his voice and shouted,
Shouted with his voice over Prilip's plain:
Herd, come you hither, leave the sheep grazing.
Young herd, come hither, with your little gun.
Then Marko laughed till the castle quivered:
Now we shall see, we shall be instructed.
When the shepherd came, old Marko seized his gun,
Throwing it about as tho' it were a feather.
And that you say can send a hero into darkness!
Take your foolish gun, there is my hand for you!
Let the ball fly and I shall catch it!
But the ball flew forth and bored thro' Marko's hand.
Then he grew pale, the old, great-hearted hero,
Sitting there in silence, his arms upon the table.
At nightfall he went and returned no more.

There is a story told by the people,
That Marko hides between the lofty mountains,
Near to the chasm of Demir-Kapia,
Where the river Vardar turns like a serpent.
There does the hero slumber thro' the centuries;
In the soil before it has he plunged his lance
And against the lance the hero-horse is fastened,
Thus to be ready for the gallant Marko
When he rides again in pursuit of exploits.
Now beyond the chasm winds a mountain-footpath,
When the wanderers go there, turning round they shout:
Do you live, do you live yet, the people's father, Marko?
And it is to them as tho' they heard an answer:
He lives, he lives yet, the people's father, Marko.

The Shade of the Balkans, pp. 123-125.

V

Thro' the woods he wanders, Strajil the robber-chief,
Thro' the woods he wanders, thro' the green woodlands,
The mother of the robber-chief is a mighty Balkan,
Strajil the robber-chief lives without a care,
The father of Strajil is the shadow of a beech-tree,
The camp of the robber-chief is the tender grass,
The spouse of the robber-chief is a slender rifle,
Wheresoe'er he sends her, there she does the work of him,
The children of the robber-chief are the white bullets,
Wheresoe'er he sends them, there they do the work for him,
Strajil the robber-chief lives without a care;
Wheresoe'er he wanders, wanders he in peace.

The Shade of the Balkans, pp. 95-96.

Petko Rachev Slaveykov

As the gray shadow of clouds swept over my face,
So did the centuries follow and leave no trace—
Some have come and have gone with lingering feet,
Some have clattered and raged with the battle's heat.
Out of my brooding dreams did they waken me
That I should behold mirth, laughter and tragedy.
For as I looked at the dawn in her robes of ice
I saw the flickering flames of a sacrifice,
I heard a shepherd singing the while he drove
His wayward, wandering flocks through the windless grove,
And in the gloom of a canopied oak I saw
The priest with his locks dishevelled, the father of law,
Interpreting evil and good of the distant ages,
And there he sat in the circle of bearded sages.

So fled the years—the gay to the grave gave hand,
As they, forsooth, in the dawn of the world were planned.

And then came those who made for a distant shore,
The captives they of a dream their bosoms bore,
While those who were condemned to the threshold-stones
Did curse the day, did blacken the night with groans.
Yet some who journeyed journeyed back again—
Of thousands one. Ah! the dreamers lying slain
Were given life in the song which the minstrel told,
And yet the fires of the heart of the land were cold,
And seldom now did the smoke of an altar rise
To wander and lose its way to the silent skies.

So fled the years—the gay to the grave gave hand,
As they, forsooth, in the dawn of the world were planned.

And then I heard the clash and the clangour of fight,—
I looked where storms had driven the clouds in flight,
I looked and saw where blood was upon the world,
How murderous brother was against brother hurled,
And how the hand of a son had seized a dart

Remorselessly to thrust in a father's heart.
Ah! so in death they sank, for a God they died
Who once on a wooden cross was crucified.
Thus over the world did Plague and Famine roam,
In towns, in villages they made their home,
But hollow tree and cave of the mountain side
Were sought of hermits gaunt, grim, savage-eyed,
For whom the world was a place of hate, and they
Groped for a day that loomed beyond their day,
Whence vanities and splendour should be cast—
But it was in their souls that I saw them fast,
Unto the grave were all their longings turned,
Nor heeded they the love that in me burned.

So fled the years—the gay to the grave gave hand,
As they, forsooth, in the dawn of the world were planned.

Then red battalions burst across the plain,
And there is none to thrust them back again.
In bonds of slavery the land is bent,
Upon its life the curse of its life is sent.
The land is dark with the vapour of burning towns,
From every rock the ravenous vulture frowns,
By desolate roads, through the glimmering forest glen
I saw the long procession of murdered men,
I heard those weep who wept at being born,
And those who from the mother's breast were torn.
I looked, and behold the fateful ravens flew,
I looked at the fields aglare with a crimson dew—
Altars were prone and the sacrificial smoke
Rose out of the flowing blood of the slaughtered folk.
So then the years did sleep where they used to tread,
For thus it is when the soul of the land is dead—
The land is forgotten of Time, it is cast behind,
There to foul as a corpse that is thrown to the wind.

So fled the years—the gay to the grave gave hand,
As they, forsooth, in the dawn of the world were planned.

And softly then as the stars to the twilight sing
So sleep came into the voice of the mountain-king.
But there was a trailing sigh and a swarm of shades
Fluttered across the gloom of the woodland glades
And then it was that another voice replied
And that was a sacred voice to the countryside,
To field and woods in delicate robes of white
Toying with dreams in the lap of the summer night:

Balkan, our father Balkan, have eyes of grace,
Harshly dost thou look from the judgment place.
What of our mothers now, of the tears they brought
To blot away the sins which the fathers wrought?
Look on those who look upon thee from the graves—
Did they live no life save the life of slaves?
Had their children naught save the milk of slaves?
Had their souls no thought save the thoughts of slaves?
Behold the wounds that out of our bosoms stream!
Count the numberless heroes who fell for a dream!
In thy crevasses, there on the rugged heights
We, thy sons, have died in a hundred fights—
But yet we awakened Time and we urged him on,
We drew the curtain of night and the daylight shone.
Now turn thy glance to the queen of the mountain throng,
Hear thou the music of swords, hear thou of songs the song!
Thither the people fly, for liberty lies in chain,
Thither we fly, the dead, to the glorious place again.
Ah! we have risen, we ride from a shadowy shore
To see the fate that our country shall have in store.

And softly then as the stars to the twilight sing
So slept the voice that spoke to the mountain-king.
And as he looked to the gloom of the woodland glades
Away they flew, the fluttering swarm of shades,
The chin of the Balkan dropped and his lips were dumb
And he was sunk in a dream of the days to come.

                              The Shade of the Balkans, pp. 29-32.

Khristo Botev

HADJI DIMITAR

He's alive, living! There on the Balkan,
Blood all bespattered, lies he a-moaning.
Hero sore wounded there in his bosom,
Hero, young lad, but a man in his prowess.

There is his rifle, dropped where he faltered,
There is his sword, all broken asunder.
Dark grow his eyes, his body is trembling
With his lips cursing all that's around him.

There lies the hero. There in the heavens
Blazes the sunlight, showing no mercy.
No healing water comes to that meadow.
Yet his warm blood is flowing e'er faster.

This is the harvest! Sing, O you slave girls,
Songs of your burden! Sun, blaze more fiercely
On this slave land. There he will perish,
Hero unrivalled. Heart, do be silent.

He who has fallen fighting for freedom,
He will not perish; all will assist him,
Earth and the heavens, creature and nature.
Singers will render songs in his honor.

Wings of the eagle bar off the sunlight;
Softly the wolf comes, licks where he's wounded.
O'er him a falcon, bird of a hero;
Thou art his brother, care for the hero.

Evening is coming—moonlight will warm him.
Stars will shine out on heaven's broad ranges.
Mountains are stirring, blowing the breezes.
Hayduk bold songs now rise from the Balkan.

Nymphs are appearing, clad in white raiment,
Wonderful, charming songs are they singing.
Softly they're tramping through the green meadow,
Come to the hero, sit down beside him.

One with sweet herbs his wounds now is binding,
This one comes up with water refreshing.
This one is kissing lips that deserve it
And he awakes, he speaks and he's smiling.

Tell me, my sister, of Karadjata?
Where is my loyal, faithful *druzhina?*
Tell me, receive then from me my spirit.
Sister, I want so also to perish.

Clasping their hands as if they were embracing,
Singing, they're flying up to the heavens,
Flying and singing, far as they're sighted,
Seeking the spirit of Karadjata.

Now there is sadness. And on the Balkan
Lies the great hero, bleeding severely,
And his cruel wounds a wolf now is licking
While the hot sun is blazing more fiercely.

C. A. M.

THE SHARING

In feeling we two are close brothers.
Like thoughts we conceal in our hearts.
I know that for naught in our lifetime
We twain will repent of our parts.

If that is correct or is evil,
Posterity is to decide.
But now with our hands stoutly clasping,
We move ever forward in stride.

We walked as one man through our lifetime,
Through suffering, exile and need,
But yet as close brothers we shared it.
Again we will share it, give heed.

We'll share all the ignorant censures,
We'll suffer the laughter of fools,
We'll suffer with never a murmur
The torturer's cruelest tools.

Our heads we shall never, no, never,
Bend low to the idols men hold.
We've spoken our hearts to each other
In songs that are sad and yet bold.

So now with our thoughts and our feelings,
We twain will move on to our fates,
We'll go to our final decision,
Till death, brother, death, we are mates.

C. A. M.

A PRAYER

O, my God, Thou Lord of Justice—
Not the one in far off heaven—
But thou, God, who dwell'st within me,
In my heart and in my doing.

Not the one who out of mud balls
Made a man and then a woman,
Whom he left, enslaved, to suffer,
Bound in chains and bent with labor.

Nor the one who asks submission,
Makes us cringe and say our prayers,
Feeds our hearts with empty stories
Of gold mansions and white stairs.

But my God of mind and reason,
Champion bold of slaves and pris'ners,
Whose Great Day of liberation
Soon shall dawn for all the nations,

Kindle in me, God Almighty,
Burning love for human freedom,
Help me fight with dauntless courage
The enslavers of my people.

Strengthen my right hand, O Father,
When the slaves arise from slumber;
Make me one of Thy bold warriors;
Take my life—give others freedom.

R. H. Markham, *Meet Bulgaria,* p. 216
(Stanzas 2, 4, 6, 10 omitted.)

Ivan Vazov

THE PINE TREE

Below the Great Balkan, a stone's throw from Thrace,
  Where the mountain, majestic and straight as a wall,
Lifts his terrible back—in a bird-haunted place
  Where green boughs are waving, white torrents appall.

With yellowing marbles, with moldering eaves,
  Mute rises the cloister, girt round with the hills
And mingling its gloom with the glimmer of leaves,
  The newness of blossoms, the murmur of rills.

Without the white walls what commotion and whirr!
  Within them how solemn, how startling the hush!
All is steeped in a slumber that nothing can stir—
  Not the waterfall shattered to foam in its rush.

In that hallowed enclosure, above the quaint shrine,
  With angel and martyr in halo and shroud,
Looms a giant-limbed tree—a magnificent pine,
  Whose black summit is plunged in the soft summer cloud.

As the wings of an eagle are opened for flight,
  As a cedar of Lebanon shields from the heat,
So he shoots out his branches to left and to right,
  Till they shade every tomb in that tranquil retreat.

The monk with white beard saw him ever the same—
  Unaltered in grandeur, in height or in girth!
Nor can anyone living declare when that frame
  Was first lifted in air, or the root pierced the earth.

That mysterious root that had long ceased to grow,
  Sunken deep in that soil—who can tell where it ends?
That inscrutable summit what mortal can know?
  Like a cloud, with the limitless azure it blends.

And perchance the old landmark, by ages unbent,
  Is sole witness to valor and virtue long past.
Peradventure he broods o'er each mighty event
  That once moved him to rapture or made him aghast.

And 'tis thus he lives on, meeting storm after storm
  With contempt and defiance—a stranger to dread.
Nor can winter or summer, that all things transform,
  Steal the plumes from his shaggy and resolute head.

From the crotches and tufts of those wide-waving boughs,
  Blithe birds by the hundreds are pouring their lays;
There in utter seclusion their nestlings they house,
  Far from envy and hate passing halcyon days.

Last of all save the mountain, the Balkan's own son
  Takes the tinge of the sunset. A crown as of fire
First of all he receives from the new-risen one,
  And salutes his dear guest with the small feathered choir.

But alas! in old age, though with confident heart
　He yet springs toward the zenith, majestic and tall—
Since he too of a world full of peril is part,
　The same fate hath found him that overtakes all.

On a sinister night came the thunder's long roll;
　No cave of the mountain but echoed that groan.
All at once fell the storm upon upland and knoll
　With implacable fury aforetime unknown.

The fields were deserted, the valleys complained;
　The heavens grew lurid with flash after flash;
In the track of the tempest no creature remained—
　Only terror and gloom and the thunderbolt's crash.

As of old, the huge tree his assailant repays
　With intense indignation, with thrust after thrust;
Till uprooted, confounded, his whole length he lays,
　With a heart-rending cry of despair, in the dust.

As a warrior attacked without warning rebounds
　Undismayed from each stroke of his deadliest foe—
Then staggers and languishes, covered with wounds,
　Knowing well that his footing he soon must forego;

As he still struggles on in the enemy's grasp,
　Falling only in death, yielding only to fate
With a final convulsion, a single deep gasp,
　That at last he survive not his fallen estate—

So the pine-tree, perceiving the end of his reign,
　Yet unsplintered, uncleft in that desperate strife,
Vouchsafed not to witness the victor's disdain,
　But with dignity straightway relinquished his life.

He is fallen! he lies there immobile, august;
　Full of years, full of scars, on the greensward he lies.
Till last evening so proudly his summit he thrust,
　To the wonder of all men, far into the skies.

And behold, as the conqueror closes the fray
  With one mortal stroke more to his down-trodden foe,
Then ignoring the conquest, all honors would pay,
  Shedding tears for the hero his hand hath brought low—

Thus the whirlwind, forgetting his fury, grew dumb,
  Now that prone on the earth his antagonist lay;
And revering the victim his stroke had o'ercome,
  To profound lamentation and weeping gave way.

Lucy C. Bull, Columbia Course in Literature,
Vol. 10, pp. 576-578.

NIGHT IN THE MONASTERY OF RILO

The moon is rising o'er the Royal peak.
The rivers storm along, then go to sleep.
The buildings breathe their quiet ancient soul
And unknown legends through our minds now creep.

Khrel's tower stands outlined against the sky.
The church's splendid domes now shine in silv'ry light.
And we can mark amid the moon's bright rays
How all the evening prayers cut through the shades of night.

'Tis quiet, yes, and strange. The soul can dream
And recreate those ancient days so fair,
Can revel sweetly in fond memories
Or rise unnoticed to the upper air.

'Tis quiet, yes, and strange. The moon shines out,
The heavens sleep. The streams sing their low song,
Night's poem lures with its entrancing spell
And far from wakeful eyes sleep tarries long.

C. A. M.

TO BULGARIA

No, I do not think that in that time
You will sacrifice yourself for gold;
Your day will shine,
Your wings unfold.

Greatness shall burn
Anew in a new century
And the sun will turn
Its smile upon your unity.

Nations at your feet will bow,
Homeland, beloved and fair,
Then. . . . But listen now!
In that morning I shall not be there.

Arthur P. Coleman
Slavonic and East European Review
Vol. 9, p. 208.

Pencho Slaveykov

A MAD PLAYER

In the presence of the Cadi
Were the villagers assembled.
Said they: "Venerable Cadi,
Sit you there with legs contorted,
But give uncontorted judgment.
Thro' the summer have we suffered
And we can endure no longer—
One mad fellow in the village
Plays and plays upon his flute,
Plays from daybreak until evening,
So that we are sore afflicted.
Maidens and young married women
Leave their work and follow him,

And at evening when we come
From our labour in the fields
We go hungrily to bed,
For that cursed song of his
Lures the soberest of housewives
From the cooking of our suppers,
And the bread—it barely rises."
Then the Cadi sat contorted
And gave uncontorted judgment.
"Bring him in," the Cadi cries,
But he enters not alone,
For the flute is on his girdle
And a ram upon his shoulder,
Ram with wondrous, silken hair
Which he lays before the Cadi.
"Well! so let us hear the flute,
That accursed instrument,
Which makes all the people mad,
And old men and women young."
So the youth began to play
And the Cadi stared at him,
Stared and started from his seat,
Sprang upon the floor and lo!
He was dancing, dancing, dancing!
"Play, mad fellow, play," cried he,
"Verily, it comes from God
And I—am I here to judge
Almighty God's immortal gift.

Henry Bernard
The Shade of the Balkans, pp. 222-223.

DREAM OF HAPPINESS

My heart is now a stranger to the world.
It's like a ruined temple from the past
And secret watchers with their jealous eyes
Into its sacred shrine their visions cast.

It sees those looks and only death expects.
It's like a ruined temple from the past.
The world's loud murmur seeks to enter in
But only to profane the noble past.

*   *   *

Dry and yellow autumn leaves
Are burned up in fires of autumn.
I tread on them and pass by them,
Yellow leaves all dry and fallen.
What they whisper, who can tell,
Yellow leaves all dry and fallen.
I will know for in the future
I shall burn in fires of autumn.

*   *   *

Waking and asleep,
I see you ever stay,
Wondrous as the night,
Clear as is the day.

Day disturbs my heart,
And I long for night.
Nights I lie and dream,
Begging daylight bright.

*   *   *

While we are young, the golden sun will warm.
The heart will cherish golden dreams which swarm.
While we are young, the path of life is pleasant
And light are those world troubles ever present.

While we are young, all things are light to bear
And sorrow is not to the heart a snare.
And then we find that joy from sorrow's sprung,
While we are young, Oh, yes, while we are young.

*   *   *

A lonely grave, a lonely vale,
The wilderness around is still.
I long have known that lonely vale,
That lonely grave beneath a hill.

I know that in that lonely grave
Deep in that lonely vale to lie
A loving hand has buried deep
An unloved orphan with a sigh.
Now for that life unwanted, dead,
For that unwanted life that's still,
A lonely grave, a lonely vale,
The wilderness around is still.

C. A. M.

Peyu Yavorov

SPRING

The snows of March are melting fast,
The village brooks but yesterday all wrapped in ice and frost
Rush fresh and overthrow their banks;
The poplars stir in the spring breeze.

From early morn the heated sun
Still warms the more from out the bluish vault of heaven clear.
The bird on high sends out its song
And greets the spring with song so sweet.

On every side there's life and stir;
The meadow wakes beneath the swarms of gay and
laughing youths,
The fields are trampled down by throngs
Of peasants glad to work again.

C. A. M.

I LOVE YOU

I love you. You are fair as heaven in your blooming youth
just as an angel's dream of love.
You are a dream that shows to me the quiet joy of truth
along that joyless path I move
and that first step toward a confession calls my heart
to sob for sin and love
and that is day and darkness is a part.

I love you, for you swim in semidarkness now
along a way uncharted, drear.
I think that you are She, that there is lurking
the erring spirit of the year
and in the gloomy ocean I now sit in pain
and turn my gaze on you
and I must know the dread abyss of fear.

I love you now—because you still can smile
before that terrorizing fate
and there is none to warn the storm-tossed bark,
no blast to bid you wait
and never do I meet "that's why I love you"
reproach or plea to wait,
while I wrong you, myself and fate.

C. A. M.

THE CALL

All silent roams the ghastly shade of death
and casts upon the earth her mantle white
her breath blows sharp amid the night
upon the snowy plains dry leaves now meet our sight.

I think of thee, dear mother. Thou art there
deep in the ravening maw of the stout earth.
I long for you, dear mother, now you're there
on that hid path. I cannot know its goal or worth.

And everywhere moves on the shade of death
and fills the graves from hoar eternity
and silently it works along with night
and silently it pushes on unto eternity.

I know that you are cold, dear mother, there,
in the dark earth with all its soulless lairs.
I dread, dear mother, also what is there
Where dreamless thought with bitter draughts the
soul embraces.

The shades of death beheld, now check their course
in heaven behind the fog the moon shines dark
a mighty call is borne along the night
the gloom increases, seeking me as its own mark.

C. A. M.

Notes

NOTES FOR CHAPTER ONE

1. Dvornik, F., *Les Slaves, Byzance et Rome au IX Siècle*, Paris, 1926. Pp. 15-16.

2. Cf. Rambaud, A., *L'Empire Grec au Dixième Siècle*, Paris, 1870. Pp. 227-230.

3. The terms "Bulgaria—Bulgarian" are derived from the old Turko-Tatar tribal name which is related not to the name of the river Volga but to the old Turk *bulgar*—"mongrel." Cf. Vasmer, Max, *Russisches Etymologisches Wörterbuch*. Heidelberg, Carl Winter, 1915. P. 102.

4. Cf. Halecki, Oscar, *Borderlands of Western Civilization*, New York, Ronald Press, 1952. Pp. 23-25.

5. Cf. Potocek, Cyril S., *Saint Cyril and Methodius*, New York, P. Y. Kennedy & Sons, 1941. P. 65.

6. The veneration of these Slavic Apostles is widely spread also in the United States, not only among the Slavic Orthodox Churches but also in the Catholic Church of both the Byzantine-Slavic Rite and also the Latin Rite; cf. the Seminary of SS. Cyril and Methodius, Orchard Lake, Mich.

7. Paszkiewicz, Henryk, *The Origin of Russia*, New York, Philosophical Library, 1954. Pp. 381-404.

8. Vlassovsky, Ivan, *Outline History of the Ukrainian Orthodox Church*, New York, 1956. Vol. I, p. 21.

9. Isajiw, Peter, *From Where did Rus-Ukraine Accept Christianity?* Philadelphia, Penn., 1952; Koch, Hans. "Byzanz, Ochrid und Kiev," *Kyrios*, Vol. I, p. 19.

10. Cf. Runciman, Steven, *A History of the First Bulgarian Empire*, London, 1930. Bobchev, S.S. "Bulgaria under Tsar Simeon," *Slavonic Review*, Vol. VII-VIII (1928-1930); Spinka, Matthew, *A History of Christianity in the Balkans. A Study in the Spread of Byzantine Culture among the Slavs*, Chicago, 1933; Black, Cyril E. "The Balkan Slavs in the Middle Ages," *A Handbook of Slavic Studies*, Cambridge, Mass., Harvard University, 1949.

11. Cf. Hrushevsky, Michael, *A History of Ukraine*, edited by O. J. Frederiksen, New Haven, Yale University Press, 1941. Pp. 59-61.

12. Cf. Vernadsky, George, *Kievan Russia*, New Haven, Yale University Press, 1948. P. 320.

13. Mishew, D. *The Bulgarians in the Past*, Lausanne, 1919. Pp. 84-85.

14. Cf. Hrycak, Paul. *The Duchy of Halych-Volynia*, New York, Shevchenko Scientific Society, 1958. P. 81.

15. Cf. Palmer, I. A. B. "The Origin of Janissaries," *Bulletin John Ryland's Library*, 35 (1953). Janissary means in Turkish "new army."

16. *Kiliynaya* school—cloister or parochial school.

17. *Rayah*—a Turkish term of contempt for the Christians.

18. *Chorbadji* was the Turkish title of the commander of a Janissary battalion in the rank of colonel or major. Later the Turks used this title

187

for Bulgarian notables in contrast to the common man in the street. As a result the title acquired in Bulgaria the significance of "quisling, collaborator, traitor."

19. Mishew D., *op. cit.*, p. 231.

20. From the Hungarian *hajdu*, "yeoman, free peasant." In the languages of the Balkan Slavs "a guerilla partisan against the Turks, avenging the oppression of the Christian population." In Bulgarian and Serbian folklore they are celebrated as heroes.

NOTES FOR CHAPTER TWO

1. *Glagol*—Old Bulgarian "word."

2. Cf. the material in Vernadsky, George, *Ancient Russia*. New Haven, Yale University Press, 1943. Pp. 345-353.

3. Murko, M. *Geschichte der Ältesten Suedslawischen Literaturen*. Leipzig, 1908.

4. Cf. Sharenkoff, V. N., *A Study of Manichaeism in Bulgaria*. New York, Columbia University Press, 1927. Obolensky, D., "The Bogomils," *Eastern Church Quarterly*, October-December, 1945.

5. Jagić, V., *History of Serbo-Croatian Literature*. Vienna, 1871. Pp. 82-90.

6. Mishew, D., *op. cit.*, p. 117.

7. Florinsky, Michael T., *Russia*, Vol. I. New York, The Macmillan Co., 1935. P. 165.

NOTES FOR CHAPTER THREE

1. Note the grammatical irregularities. Paisi often wavers between strict and popular usage, since he had no contemporary standards on which to rely.

2. Cf. Jacques Lacarrière, *Mount Athos*: Holy Mountain. P. Seghers, Paris, 1954.

NOTES FOR CHAPTER FOUR

1. There was a lengthy correspondence between Koraes and Thomas Jefferson.

2. Yury Venelin (1802-1839) was a Ukrainian scholar born in the Carpathian region. He was the son of a priest and studied theology in Lviv. The Bulgarian colonists in Bessarabia aroused his interest in the Bulgarian cause.

In 1825, he went to Moscow, joined the Slavophiles and won their support for the freedom of Bulgaria. He published books on Bulgarian grammar, history and folksongs. His most popular work was *Old and New Bulgarians* (1827). He died before he had a chance to visit Bulgaria.

3. Orthodox priests used the title of pope. At this period the rules of patronymics and family names in Bulgaria had few settled rules.

4. In the Russian original, the bird is a swan.

5. Hrytsko Kvitka-Osnovyanenko (1778-1843) was the father of the Ukrainian novel. He wrote sentimental and humorous tales on the life of the peasants and popular plays. His novel *Marusia* won popularity in France in an excellent translation and appeared in English with an introduction by John Buchan.

6. Taras Shevchenko (1814-1861) was the national bard of Ukraine. He formed the modern Ukrainian nationalism by proclaiming as the ideal of Ukraine "the new and just law of George Washington." He was also a distinguished painter and etcher.

7. Bishop Josef Strossmayer (1815-1905) was the founder of the Croatian Academy of Liberal Arts and Sciences in Zagreb. He was the political leader of the Croatians and an advocate of the unity of all Southern Slavs.

8. Marko Vovchok (1834-1907), pen name of Maria Vilinska-Markovych. She lived in Paris and St. Petersburg and wrote in a beautiful Ukrainian language stories protesting against oppression, especially serfdom.

9. Mykola Kostomariv (1817-1885) was a professor in the Universities of Kiev and St. Petersburg, a Ukrainian writer and historian, organizer of the Brotherhood of SS. Cyril and Methodius (1845) and the author of its ideology; cf. Sydoruk, John P., *Ideology of the Cyrillo-Methodians and its Origins.* Winnipeg-Chicago, 1954. *Slavistika.* No. 19.

NOTES FOR CHAPTER SIX

1. George Washburn (1833-1915) joined the newly established Robert College (1864) as Professor of Philosophy in 1868. He was Acting President, 1870-1877 and President, 1877-1903. For his services, he received the thanks of the First Bulgarian Parliament and in 1884 was decorated by Prince Alexander with the Order of St. Alexander.

2. Cf. Mishew, D., *op. cit.,* pp. 318-319.

3. Cf. Gladstone, W. E., *The Bulgarian Horrors and the Eastern Question, Lessons from the Massacres and the Conduct of the Turkish Government towards Bulgaria.*

NOTE FOR CHAPTER SEVEN

1. According to Cizevsky (*Comparative Slavic Literature*, p. 118), the negative type of Bulgarian petty-bourgeois Bay Ganyu was created under the influence of the Russian humorist N. A. Lejkin.

NOTES FOR CHAPTER EIGHT

1. Drahomaniv in Switzerland bitterly opposed George Plekhanov (1857-1918), the father of Russian Marxist imperialism. In this connection he published articles praising the Irish struggle against British imperialism and offered them as a model for Ukrainian action.

2. Lesya Ukrainka (1872-1913) was the most prominent Ukrainian poetess. Because of ill health, she travelled widely in the warmer climates, and her views, which had much to do with the formation of modern Ukrainian nationalism, are now being falsified by the Soviets. A number of her works in English translation by Percival Cundy were published in New York (*Spirit of Flame,* New York, Bookman Associates, 1950).

3. *Chetnik*—a member of an armed and trained body of men fighting for freedom.

NOTES FOR CHAPTER ELEVEN

1. *Bulgarian Poets,* edited by D. Markov, Moscow, 1952, p. 14.

2. *Ibid.,* p. 19.

Selected Bibliography

ARNAUDOV, M. "Shevchenko a bolharska literatura" (Shevchenko and the Bulgarian Literature), T. Shevchenko, *Tvory*, Vol. XV, pp. 209-235, ed. by Roman Smal-Stocki. Warsaw-Lviv, 1938 (Ukrainian).

BADEV, IORDAN. "Bulgarian Literature," *Encyclopaedia Britannica*, Vol. IV, p. 368, Edition, 1951.

————. *Skitsi na zhivite* (Sketches of the Living). Sofia, 1934 (Bulgarian).

BRISBY, L. "Bulgarian Writers and their Mentors," *Soviet Survey*, No. 25, pp. 23-28. London, 1958.

Bulgarski Pisateli—Jivot, Tvorchestvo, Ideit (Bulgarian Writers, Life, Works, Ideas), ed. M. Arnaudov. Sofia, 1929 (Bulgarian).

"Bulgarian Writers Revolt," *East Europe*, Vol. VII, No. 3, pp. 15-23.

"Bulgarian Writers Revolt," Texts and Documents, *ibid.*, Vol. VII, No. 5, pp. 50-56.

Bulgarskiye Poety, ed. by D. Markov. Moscow, 1952 (Russian).

DSAKALOVA-DUMAS, VALERIE. *Conteurs bulgares d'aujourd'hui, récits, contes, nouvelles, choisis et adaptés,* with a preface by Nicholai Dontchov. Sofia, 1937.

DERJAVIN, KONST. *Bolgarsky Teatr* (Bulgarian Theatre). Moscow, Leningrad, 1950 (Russian).

DONTCHOV, NICOLAI. *Esquisses d'un tableau de la nouvelle littérature bulgare,* with a preface by Frank L. Schoell. Sofia, 1935.

————. *Influences étrangères dans la littérature bulgare,* with a preface by Marcel Bion. Sofia, 1934.

GALABOFF, KONSTANTIN. "Die neuere bulgarische Literatur." *Deutsche Rundschau*, No. 216, pp. 223-234. Berlin, 1928.

HATEAU, GEORGES. *Panorama de la littérature bulgare contemporaine*. Paris 1937.

MANDRYKA, M. I. *Z bolharsko-ukrayinskykh literaturnykh vzayemyn, Vplyv Shevchenka na bolharsku poeziyu* (A Phase of

Selected Bibliography 191

Bulgarian-Ukrainian Literary Relations. Shevchenko's Influence on Bulgarian Poetry), *Slavistika*, No. 26. Winnipeg, 1956 (Ukrainian).

MANNING, CLARENCE A. "Communism and Bulgarian Literature," *American-Bulgarian Review*, Vol. V, No. 2, pp. 5-6. New York, 1954.

————. "Literature of Balkan Slavs," *Handbook of Slavic Studies*, ed. by Leonid I. Strakhovsky. Cambridge, Mass., 1949.

————, "The Modern Scene in Bulgaria," *Books Abroad*, Vol. XIV, pp. 237-239. Norman, Okla., 1940.

MARKHAM, R. H. *Meet Bulgaria*. Sofia, 1931.

PENEV, BOYAN. *Istoriya na novata bulgarska literatura* (History of the Modern Bulgarian Literature), 4 vol. Sofia, 1932 (Bulgarian).

————. *Bulgarska Literatura* (Bulgarian Literature). Sofia, 1930 (Bulgarian).

SHISHMANOV, DIMITAR. *La Mouvement littéraire en Bulgarie*. Sofia, 1925.

————. *A Survey of Bulgarian Literature*, tr. by Clarence A. Manning. Williamsport, Pa., 1932.

Razvitiye na bolgarska literatura (Development of Bulgarian Literature), ed. Panteley Zarev and Ognyan Boyardjiyev, 3 vols. Sofia, 1952 (Bulgarian).

The Shade of the Balkans, ed. Henry Bernard. London. 1904.

VASILEV, ST. "Die bulgarische Literaturgeschichte und Literaturkritik in den Jahren 1924-1929," *Zeitschrift für Slavische Philologie*, Vol. VIII, pp. 443-463; Vol. IX, 165-195, 426-452. Berlin, 1932-1933.

Index

Aegean Sea, 11, 46
Aesop, 65
Akir the Wise, 34
Aksakov, Ivan, 67-68
Albania, 41, 130, 153
Albanian language, 31
Albigenses, 18
Alexander the Great, 12, 34
Alexander I, tsar of Russia, 54
Alexander II, tsar of Russia, 68, 82, 114, 151, 153
Alexander, Prince, of Battenberg, 71, 82, 84
Alexander Nevsky, St., 150
Alexandria, 34
Alexis, tsar of Moscow, 27
Altaic languages, 12, 13, 30
American Bible Society, 57, 66, 81
Anatolia, 34
Andrew, St., 49
Angelov, B., 134
Apocrypha, 34, 35
Aprilov, V., 55-57
Arabia, 34
Arabs, 12
Archer, 134
Aristotle, 34
Armenians, 21
Arsen Tsrnoyevich, patriarch, 26
Asen, Bulgarian dynasty, 71
Asperukh, Bulgar khan, 12
Athanasius of Alexandria, 33
Athens, 37, 59, 139
Athos, Mount, 23, 24, 31, 45-48, 58
Austria, 25 ff., 48 f., 60, 66, 95
Avars, 14
Avramov, R., 160

Badev, I., 142
Bagdad, 130
Bagryana, E., 136
Bakunin, M., 74, 75
Balkan Mts., 13
Balmont, K., 118
Baltic Sea, 13

Balzac, H., 125
Bansko, 57
Baronius, Caesar, 48
Basil the Macedonian, emperor, 17
Baudelaire, C., 127
Beethoven, L. von, 110
Belcheva, M., 137
Belev, Kh., 150
Belgium, 83
Belgrade, 26, 52, 60, 62-71
Belo-Ruthenians, 12, 41
Belorussians, 31
Berlin, 119, 130
Berne, 104, 119
Beron, P., 55 f.
Bessarabia, 59, 82
Black Bulgary, 12
Black Sea, 11-14, 27, 53
Blagoyev, D., 145 ff.
Bogomils, 18 f., 35-38, 135, 137, 149
Bogorov, I., 61 f.
Bohemia, 15
Bolgrad, 59 f.
Boris, khan and tsar, 14-19, 32
Boris II, tsar of Bulgaria, 131-132, 146 ff., 154
Boris, St., of Ruce, 18
Borotbisty, 155
Borovan, 76
Bosnia, 20, 35, 83
Botev, Kh., 41, 69-80, 83-87, 94, 117, 154, 163
Bradati, Joseph, 51
Braila, 62, 70-75, 84
Brashov, 55 f.
British Bible Society, 57, 60
Brotherhood of Sts. Cyril and Methodius, 69
Bucharest, 54-84, *passim*
Budapest, 48, 68
Buddha, 34
Bulgaria, state and people, 1 ff.; horde, 12 ff.; first empire, 16 ff., 31 ff., 143; second empire, 19 ff., 37 ff.; under Turkish rule, 21 ff.,

42 ff.; principality, 82 ff.; independent, 83 ff.; Communist, 152 ff.
Bulgarian Eagle, 61
Bulgarian Church, 14 ff.
Bulgarian Exarchate, 72 ff.
Bulgarian Morning Star, 62
Bulgarian National Theatre, 123, 128, 135, 141 f., 155 ff.
Bulgarska, Zora, 70
Byron, G. G., 53, 74, 88, 124
Byzantine (Eastern Roman) Empire, 11 ff., 35 ff., 141 ff., *passim*

Camus, A., 161
Carpathian Mts., 41
Caspian Sea, 14
Cathari, 18
Caucasus, 13, 30
Chalcidice, 46
Chalki, 24, 57
Charles XII, king of Sweden, 27
Chataldja, 130
Chernyshevsky, N., 67 f., 74, 101
Chervenkov, V., 157-9
Chicago, 98 f.
Chilingirov, S., 142
Chiprovets, 26, 51
Chirpan, 115
Chrysostom, St., 32 f.
Church Slavic Language, 15, 18, 32, 38
Chuvash language, 12
Clement of Rome, St., 15, 32, 42
Clement of Okhrida, St., 32
Commentaries on Gospel, etc., 33
Communists, 86, 95, 117, 131 ff.
Constance, 37
Constantine the Great, emperor, 21
Constantine the Philosopher, (Cf. St. Cyril), 15, 31
Constantine XI Paleologue, 21
Constantinople, 11-131, *passim.*
Constantinople News, 61
Cossacks, 31
Court of Law for the people, 33
Crete, 62
Crimea, 27
Croatia, 31, 41
Crusaders, 19, 46

Cumans, 19
Cyril, St., (Cf. Constantine the Philosopher), 15 ff., 31 ff., 56
Cyrillic script, 30, 35
Czechoslovakia, 122

Dalmatia, 31
Damascene the Studite, 38
Dante, 35, 97
Danube River, 11 ff., 19 ff., 54, 70, 74 ff.
Danubian Principalities, 27, 53
Dardanelles, 13
Debelyanov, D., 132 f.
Delchev, 115, 117
Delo, 115 f.
Digenis, 34
Dimitrov, G., 150 ff.
Djordjevich, P., 26
Dnieper River, 13, 17
Dobrolyubov, N., 67, 74
Dobrudja, 11, 82, 120, 136, 138, 152 ff.
Dobrych, 136
Dostoyevsky, F., 35
Doyran, 100
Drahomaniv, M., 114, 139, 164
Drumev, V. (Klement Branitski), 71, 128
Dudintsev, 158

Eastern Rumelia, 82 ff.
Egypt, 34
Elena, 100, 119
Elin Pelin (D. Ivanov), 125 ff.
Engels, F., 119
England, 18
Epiphanius of Cyprus, 33
Evthymi (Euthymius), patriarch, 37

Ferdinand, emperor of Austria, 26
Ferdinand, tsar of Bulgaria, 83, 98, 131, 146, 156
Filotey, 43
Filov, B., 153
Flame (Plamuk), 157 ff.
Flaubert, G., 125
Florence, 96
Fotinov, K., 60 f.
France, 13, 18, 20, 62, 100, 119, 130
Franciscans, 35

Franko, I., 119
Franks, 13

Gabe, D., 136
Gabrovo, 55 ff., 97
Galabov, K., 134
Galakhov, 65
Galatz, 70, 84
Ganev, D., 160
Garibaldi, 74
Gaul, 13
Geneva, 114, 116, 139
Genov, T., 158 ff.
Georgiev, M., 105
Georgius Monachus, 33
Georgius Synkellus, 33
Germany, 18, 35, 60 ff., 95, 122 ff., 164
Gerov, N., 63 ff., 84
Gibraltar, 131
Gladstone, W., 81
Glagolitic script, 30
Gochev, G., 159
Goethe, J. W., 65, 108
Gogol (Hohol), N., 56, 67, 78, 101
Golden Horn, 21
Gorky, M., 155
Great Britain, 83 f., 130 f.
Greece and Greeks (Cf. Byzantine Empire), 15-72, 129, 131, 153
Gregory, Nazianzen, 33
Grenoble, 136
Grigory Tsamblak, 37
Grozev, I., 135
Gulyashki, A., 155 ff.
Gyurgevo, 74 f.

Hadji Dimitar, 77
Hadji Khristo, 53
Hadji Stephcho, 53
Hadrian II, Pope, 15
Haemus, Mt., 13
Halych-Volynia, 19
Hamartolos, 33
Hauptmann, G., 119, 121
Hayda, 66
hayduks, 26, 40 f., 76
Hebrew, 16, 32 ff.
Heine, H., 108 ff., 116, 124
Hemingway, E., 161

Hercegovina, 83
Herzen, A., 67 f.
Hesychasm, 37, 46
Hexaemeron, 34
Historical Library, 143
Hitler, A., 153
Hlib (Gleb), St., 18
Holy Roman Empire, 20
Homer, 13
Hromada, 114
Hugo, V., 96
Hungary, 14, 25 ff., 52, 157, 160
Hunnic language, 13 f.
Hunyadi, Janos, 25, 40
Hyperion, 134 ff., 149

Ibsen, H., 119, 128
Ignatyev, N., Count, 81
Illyrians, 12
Innocent III, Pope, 46
Ioakhim, 19
Ioan Exarch, 32 ff.
Ioan Rilski, St., 37, 45
Iovkov, I., 138
Iranians, 13, 18
Islam (Cf. Mohammedans, Turks), 20 ff.
Italy and Italians, 43, 89, 108
Ivan III, tsar of Moscow, 21, 27
Ivan Asen, Bulgarian emperor, 19
Izbornik of Svyatoslav, 34

Jagic, V. von, 41
Jan Sobieski, king of Poland, 26
Janissaries, 23 f.
Jena, 114
Jeravna, 138
Jeremiah, Priest, 36
John of Damascus, St., 33
Juan of Austria, Don, 26

Kalchev, K., 159
Kalfov, D., 142
Kalofer, 73 f.
Kaloyan (Kaloiannes) Asen, Bulgarian emperor, 19
Kameneva, A., 142
Karageorge, 52

Karakozov, 68
Karaliychev, A., 143
Karavelov, L., 67 ff., 84, 94, 123, 163
Karavelova, L., 116
Kareya, 48
Karima, A., 129
Karlovtsi, 26, 47 f.
Katayev, 152
Kazanluk, 104, 112
Kharkiv, 60
Khazars, 31
Kherson, 31
Khilandar Monastery, 46 ff., 58
Khmelnytsky, B., 26
Khrabar, Monk, 32
Khristov, K., 121 f.
Khrushchev, N., 157 ff.
Kiev, 14, 17, 27, 41 ff., 60 f., 71, 114
Kirikov, I., 128
Kiril, Prince, 153
Kladovo, 75
Klopstock, F. G., 35
Kobylyanska, O., 119
Komnenos, 135
Konstantin, Bishop, 32
Konstantin, Presbyter, 33
Konstantinov, A., 97 ff., 108, 146
Konstantinov, K., 141
Koprivshtitsa, 63 ff., 80, 133
Korniychuk, A., 152
Kosovo, 19, 25, 37 ff.
Kossuth, L., 70
Kostenetsky, K., 37
Kostomariv, M., 69, 78
Kostov, S. L., 141 f.
Kosma, Priest, 36 ff.
Kotel, 48, 53, 55, 58, 62, 74
Kozaks, 26
Kozloduy, 76
Kracholov, T., 115
Kraguyevats, 57
Kraikof, Y., 51
Kremlin, 87, 162
Kristev, K., 107 ff., 113 ff.
Kritika, 113
Krum, Bulgarian khan, 14, 30
Krylov, I., 64 f.
Krizhanich, J., 43
Kuchuk-Kainardji, 27
Kunev, T., 155

Kvitka-Osnovyanenko, H., 64, 78, 101
　f., 163
Kyulyakov, K., 155

Lago di Como, 108
Latin, 16 ff., 32 ff.
Lavra Monastery, 46
Lavrenti, 46
Lazar, Knez (Prince), 19, 37
Legend about the Babylonian Empire, 43
Leipzig, 61, 108 ff.
Lenin, N., 146
Lepanto, 26
Lermontov, M., 65, 74, 78, 98, 110,
　117, 124, 132
Lesya Ukrainka, 115, 120 f.
Levski, V., 69, 77, 87, 126
Liliyev, N., 135 f.
Literaturnaya Entsiklopediya, 86
Literary Front, 157 ff.
London Daily News, 81
Long, A., 66, 81
Louis the German, King, 14
Louis of Hungary, King, 25
Lovchen, 52
Lviv, 119, 148
Lyubosloviye, 60

Macedonia, 12, 31 f., 59, 66, 85, 100,
　115 ff., 130, 146
Macedonia, 66
Madara, 30
Malalas, 33 f.
Manicheanism, 18
Manov, E., 158 ff.
Maritsa River, 19, 39
Marko, King, 39 f., 65, 149
Marko Bodjar, 53
Marmora, Sea of, 24, 57
Mars, E., 128
Marseilles, 62
Marx, K., 119
Marxism, 107, 154 ff.
Massilianism, 18
Mazepa, I. Hetman, 27
McGahan, G., 81
Menea, 33
Merezhkovsky, D., 118
Methodius, St., 15 ff., 30 ff., 56

Methodius of Patara, 33
Michael III, emperor, 14 f.
Michael Asen, Bulgarian emperor, 19
Michael Obrenovich, prince of Serbia, 68
Mickiewicz, A., 111
Mikhaylovski, S., 100 f.
Mikolayiv, 97
Milton, J., 35
Miladinov brothers, D. and K., 66 f., 87
Miletich, S., 68
Milev, G., 148
Milosh Obrenovich, prince of Serbia, 52, 57
Mina of Kostur, 39
Minkov, S., 150
Misl (Thought), 109
Missolonghi, 53
Moesia, 12
Mohacs, 25
Mohammedans (Cf. Islam, Turks), 27 ff.
Moldavia, 37, 41, 53, 70
Molière, 98
Molotov, V., 150
Momchil, 149
Mongols, 43
Montenegro, 52, 130 ff.
Moravia, 15, 30 f., 42
Moscow, 27, 37, 43, 55, 67, 84 ff., 101, 154 ff.
Munich, 135
Muscovy, 21, 27, 41, 43, 49
Murad II, Ottoman sultan, 46
Mutafov, Ch., 134

Nadson, S., 117
Nancy, 118
Narodniki, 68 f., 102
Naum, St., 15
Navarino, 53
Nazis, 155
Nechayev, S., 75
Nekrasov, N., 126
Nemanya, Stepan, 47
Nemirov, D., 140, 143
Nenadovich, P., 47
Neofit Bozveli, 58 f.
Neofit Rilski, 57, 64

Neuilly, 146
New York Herald, 81
Nezavisimost, 69
Neznakomov, P., 159
Nicephorus, emperor, 14, 17
Nicholas, king of Montenegro, 132
Nietzsche, F., 108, 111, 120
Nikopol, 26
Nizhyn, 56, 60, 163
Nomocanon, 32 ff.
Novi Sad, 26, 62, 68

Odesa, 27 f., 56, 60-84, 97, 163
Odrin, 55, 66, 96 f., 130
Okhrida, 13-18, 30 ff., 41
Orbini, Mauro, 47
Ottoman Empire (Cf. Turkey), 20, 22, 27, 43, 52, 56

Paisi Khilandarski, Father, 44-59, 61, 64, 87, 144, 163
Paleia, 33
Pan-Slavism, 43
Pantaleymon, St., 46
Parchevich, P., 26
Paris, 55, 98, 108, 116, 135
Paterik, 32
Paul, St., 46
Paulicianism, 18, 51
Pazvantoglou, 24
Peloponnesus, 12
Penev, B., 134
Penev, K., 159
Pereyaslavets, 17
Persia, 34
Persian Gulf, 130
Peter I, tsar of Russia, 27
Peter Asen, Bulgarian emperor, 19
Petkanov, K., 143
Phanar, 21 ff., 58
Philip of Macedon, 12
Philippi, 46
Photius, patriarch, 14
Phryne, 109
Physiologus, 34
Pilate, 42
Pirdop, 101 f.
Pirot, 112
Pisarev, D., 67, 74, 101
Plato, 33 f.

Pliska-Aboda, 12 ff.
Plovdiv, 19, 59 ff., 82 ff., 92, 96, 108, 115, 133
Poe, E. A., 126 ff.
Poland, 15, 20, 26, 41, 157, 160
Poltava, 27
Polyanov, D., 147-8
Polyanov, V., 143
Prague, 98, 119
Pravda, 86
Preslav, 14 ff., 30
Prilep, 39
Prometheus, 110
Pushkin, A., 65, 74, 78, 88, 98, 124, 135

Radevski, Kh., 158 ff.
Racho Kazandjiyata, 64
Ragusa, 47
Rakitin, I., 142
Rakovski, G. S., 48, 62 ff., 71, 87, 94, 154
Rastsvetnikov, A., 155
Raychev, G., 137
Raynov, N., 137
Rilke, R. M., 35
Rilo Monastery, 37, 57 f.
Robert College, 81
Romania, 11 f., 31 f., 53-84, 130, 138, 144, 152
Rome, 14 ff., 32, 42, 96
Rossikon Monastery, 46
Rostislav, prince of Moravia, 14 ff.
Ruce (Cf. Ukraine), 15 ff., 34, 41, 43, 49
Rumyantsev, N., 148
Ruse, 69-74, 84, 119, 140
Russia, 27 ff., 60-98, 101, 131, 155 f., 164

Salonika, 15, 31, 60, 96, 131
Samokov, 45, 48, 57
Samuel, Bulgarian tsar, 17
Saint Petersburg, 49, 54, 84
San Stefano, 82
Sandomierz, 15
Sava, St., 47
Saylovo, 125
Sazava Monastery, 15
Schopenhauer, A., 108

Schuyler, E., 81
September, 157
Serbia, state and people, 19 ff., 37 ff., 49, 59, 68, 76, 81, 130 ff., 131
Shevchenko, T., 65 ff., 77 ff., 101, 163
Shipka, 82, 87, 111
Shishmanov, D., 139 f.
Shishmanov, I., 114-116, 120, 128, 139
Sholokhov, 155
Shumen, 70 f., 103
Shushulova, P., 74
Shvarkin, 152
Siberia, 43
Simeon, Bulgarian tsar, 16, 32 f., 42
Simeon II, Bulgarian tsar, 153
Skobelev, General, 108
Slaveykov, Pencho, 107-120, 129
Slaveykov, P. R., 64-66, 84 f., 107, 163
Slavic Rite, 15 ff., 32 ff.
Sliven, 74, 136, 141
Slavania (Slavonia), 12
Slovaks, 41
Smirnensky, Kh., 148
Smyrna, 60
Society of United Slavs, 69
Sofia, 19, 26, 51, 84, 97, 100 ff., *passim*
Sofroni Vrachanski (Vladislavov, S.), 48, 53 ff.
Sophia Paleologue (Zoe), 21
Sopot, 83 f.
Spain, 150
Stalin, J., 153 ff.
Stamatov, G., 123 ff.
Stamboliyski, A., 104, 131-132, 146 ff., 154
Stambolov, S., 71, 78, 96 f.
Stara Planina, 73
Stara Zagora, 66, 82, 108, 121, 135, 137
Stefan Dushan, Serb emperor, 19, 49
Story of Solomon and Kitovras, 34
Stefanit and Ikhnilat, 34
Stoyanov, L., 134, 148-160
Stoyanov, R., 142
Strashimirov, A., 103 ff., 108, 137
Strelkov, L., 155 ff.
Strindberg, J. A., 119
Strossmayer, J., Bishop, 66
Strubel, I., 143
Svoboda, 69
Struga, 66

Suez, 131
Svilengrad, 84
Svishtov, 58, 97, 100, 135
Svyatoslav of Kiev, 17, 34
Sweden, 27, 114
Switzerland, 104, 114, 119

Takev, M., 98
Tatar-Pazardjik, 96, 103, 136
Tatars, 14
Theophilus, emperor, 33
Thessaly, 62
Third Rome, 27, 43
Thought (Cf. *Misl*), 112 ff.
Thrace, 11, 143
Tiraspol, 123
Tirnovo, 19 ff., 37, 43, 55-87, 100, 119, 137, 165
Tito, 162
Tobit, 34
Todorov, P., 119-121, 129, 133, 143
Tolstoy, L., 101, 111
Toromanski, K., 159
Totyu, F., 75
Toulouse, 119
Transylvania, 40, 55
Trayanov, T., 136, 148
Trevna, 65, 107
Troy, 34
Tsankov, A., 132
Turkey (Cf. Mohammedans, Ottoman Empire, Islam) 11-69, 129, 146

Ukraine, 12-56, *passim*, 67, 77, 102, 114, 123
Union of Soviet Socialist Republics, 150 ff.
United States of America, 98, 131, 153
Ural Mts., 14

Varlaam and Josaphat, 34
Vardalachos, P., 55
Varna, 25, 103, 135 f.
Vasilev, O., 155
Vasilev, V., 134
Vatican, 47
Vatropedi Monastery, 47
Vazov, I., 80, 83-113, *passim*, 123, 125, 128, 135, 141, 154, 164
Velichkov, K., 84, 96 ff.

Velichkov, M., 159
Venelin, Y., 56, 101
Venice, 51
Vidin, 20, 24, 54, 114
Vienna, 25 ff., 56, 60, 108-116, 135, 141
Village Conversation, 126
Vikings, 17
Vlachs, 19
Vlaykov, T. G., 101 ff.
Vola, 76
Volga River, 12, 17, 31
Volodymyr, Grand Prince of Kiev, 17 f., 43
Voltaire, 89
Vovchak, Marko, 67 f.
Voynikov, D., 70 f.
Vratsa, 53 ff., 76
Vukashin, King, 19, 39
Vyshensky, I., 46

Wallachia, 41, 53
Washburn, G., 81
Wladyslaw, king of Poland, 25
Word of the Bulgarian Emigrés, 75

Yanko of Sibiu, 40
Yantra River, 58
Yasenkov, Kh., 148
Yavorov, P., 115-119, 121, 126, 129, 133, 134
Yoasaf, 37
Yovanovich, A., 55
Yovanovich, Zmay, 68
Yugoslavia, 11, 153

Zagorchinov, S., 149 f.
Zagreb, 66
Zastava, 68
Zelich, G., 48
Zhdanov, A., 154, 160
Zhivkov, T., 160
Zidarov, K., 156, 160
Zlatorog, 134 ff.
Zlatostruy, 33
Zname, 75
Znaniye, 69
Zoe Paleologue, 21
Zographu Monastery, **46 ff.**
Zola, E., 125